Britain 1940

This book is dedicated to my late dear friend John Hudson whose interest and passion for the history of the Second World War knew no bounds.

Britain 1940

The Decisive Year on the Home Front

Anton Rippon

PEN & SWORD
HISTORY

First published in Great Britain in 2020 by
Pen & Sword History
An imprint of
Pen & Sword Books Ltd
Yorkshire – Philadelphia

ISBN 978 1 52676 770 7

Printed and bound in the UK by TJ International Ltd,
Padstow, Cornwall.

Pen & Sword Books Limited incorporates the imprints of Atlas,
Archaeology, Aviation, Discovery, Family History, Fiction, History,
Maritime, Military, Military Classics, Politics, Select, Transport,
True Crime, Air World, Frontline Publishing, Leo Cooper, Remember
When, Seaforth Publishing, The Praetorian Press, Wharncliffe
Local History, Wharncliffe Transport, Wharncliffe True Crime
and White Owl.

For a complete list of Pen & Sword titles please contact

PEN & SWORD BOOKS LIMITED
47 Church Street, Barnsley, South Yorkshire, S70 2AS, England
E-mail: enquiries@pen-and-sword.co.uk
Website: www.pen-and-sword.co.uk

Or

PEN AND SWORD BOOKS
1950 Lawrence Rd, Havertown, PA 19083, USA
E-mail: Uspen-and-sword@casematepublishers.com
Website: www.penandswordbooks.com

Contents

Introduction

I still have the dog-eared school exercise book bearing the coat-of-arms of Derby Borough Education Committee. It is dated September 1953 and my name and the word 'History' are carefully inscribed on its blue cover. Inside there are short essays – we called them 'compositions' – on various aspects of our island's story. The Battle of Hastings, Agincourt, the Spanish Armada, the wars against Napoleon, they are all here. For some reason I missed out the Great War and so there is nothing between Trafalgar, which is decorated with a coloured crayon drawing of HMS *Victory* and a blind-in-one-eye stick figure in a funny hat, and the page headed, in blue school ink straight from the inkwell, 'The Second World War'.

Alas, my account, that of a nine-year-old, is subjective and lopsided. After the briefest explanation of how Britain came to be at war in September 1939, there follows impressive coverage of 1940. It is all there – Dunkirk, the Battle of Britain, the Blitz, and more. But then, after leaving London still ablaze, I bring matters to a swift conclusion: 'The war ended in 1945 and was won by Britain.' There is no mention of El Alamein, or Burma, or D-Day. I can only imagine that I had a deadline to meet.

So 1940 has always remained the significant year in my mind. The one that coloured my childhood, growing up when bombsites were our playground, food was still rationed, and my best pal's middle name was Winston, presumably because he was born in September 1940, when the Battle of Britain had just been won, the Blitz had just begun, and another Winston had just told the nation:

'… we must regard the next week or so as a very important period in our history. It ranks with the days when the Spanish Armada was approaching the Channel, and Drake was finishing his game

of bowls; or when Nelson stood between us and Napoleon's Grand
Army at Boulogne.'

I knew that I was right to jump straight from Trafalgar to Dunkirk.

The purpose of this book is to try to shed some light on what it was
like to live in Britain throughout 1940. It does not pretend to be the
definitive account of the actions that were fought but it does aim to show
how ordinary people heard about them and reacted to them while trying
to get on with their everyday lives around blackouts, food shortages, air-
raid warnings and reminders that careless talk really did cost lives.

Anton Rippon

Prelude

'Gas masks have suddenly become part of everyday civilian life and everybody is carrying the square cardboard cartons that look as though they might contain a pound of grapes for a sick friend.'

Mollie Panter-Downes in the *New Yorker* magazine

At 2.30pm on 25 August 1939, a bomb placed in the carrier basket of a bicycle exploded in the heart of Coventry. Nine days before the Second World War began, Britain was already familiar with enemy action. By June that year, an IRA campaign known as the 'S Plan', devised to sabotage the economic, civil and military infrastructure of the United Kingdom, had launched fifty-seven bomb attacks in London and seventy in the provinces. On 16 January, 27-year-old railway porter Albert Ross was killed when a 5lb bomb – one of three – was detonated in the centre of Manchester. That day there were also bombs planted in London, Liverpool and Birmingham. The orchestrated attacks continued through the spring and summer; in the small hours of 3 July alone, bombs exploded at railway stations in Birmingham, Coventry, Derby, Leicester, Nottingham, Stafford and Warwick. On 26 July, Dr Donald Campbell, a 36-year-old lecturer in Latin at Edinburgh University, was killed when a bomb was detonated at London's King's Cross station. He was returning with his wife from their honeymoon.

The following month, the bombers returned to Coventry, and as Elsie Ansell, a 21-year-old shop assistant, paused to look in the window of a jeweller in the busy shopping area of Broadgate, the bomb in the bicycle went off. Elsie could be identified only through her clothes and her engagement ring; she had been due to marry in two weeks' time. The bomb claimed four more victims – John Arnott (15) and Rex Gentle (30) who both worked for W.H. Smith & Son, James Clay (82) who was a former president of the Coventry and District Co-operative Society, and

Gwilym Rowlands (50) who was a road sweeper. Seventy others were injured. On 12 December, five people appeared before Birmingham Assizes, charged with Elsie's murder. Husband and wife Joseph and Mary Hewitt, and Brigid O'Hara were found not guilty, but 32-year-old Peter Barnes and 29-year-old James McCormack who used the alias of James Richards were found guilty and sentenced to death. They would be hanged at Winson Green prison in Birmingham on Wednesday, 7 February 1940. Later that year Coventry would have more horrors unleashed upon it, this time from the skies.

For now, though, the last few months of 1939 – the Phoney War, the Twilight War, whatever name people cared to give it – meant that life in Britain had an almost surreal quality. After Prime Minister Neville Chamberlain had finished his broadcast on the first Sunday morning of September, everyone knew that life would now be different. They went outside to talk about it with their neighbours, made a pot of tea, ate their Sunday joint and readied themselves as best they could for whatever lay ahead. And the next few months were different – but different in an entirely unexpected way. There were no bombs from the sky and no drastic changes between the state of war that now existed and the state of emergency that had lasted all summer with its Civil Defence exercises, feverish building of Anderson shelters and general unease.

Hitler was hoping that after he had smashed Poland, Britain and her allies might sue for peace. Initially, he forbade air attacks on British civilian targets. The appalling European winter of 1939–40 meant a further delay, although German reticence did not apply to the sea. At 9pm on the first day of the war, the British liner SS *Athenia*, bound for Montreal, was sunk by a German submarine 250 miles off the Hebrides. The Germans claimed that she had been mistaken for an armed merchant vessel. The death toll of 112 included 28 Americans.

By the end of September, more than 140,000 tons of British shipping had been sunk, and on 14 October 1939 a German U-boat penetrated the British naval base at Scapa Flow in the Orkneys and torpedoed the 29,000-ton battleship HMS *Royal Oak* with the loss of 833 lives including those of 126 boy-sailors, some as young as 15. It was a truly demoralising event, coming as it did with the mighty battleship at anchor in the supposedly impregnable base. Defences had been allowed to deteriorate in peacetime with submarine netting now inadequate.

Yet if the sinking of the *Royal Oak* brought the war much closer to home, as 1939 ebbed away, life in Britain settled down and continued pretty much as normal, at least within the constraints of wartime restrictions. True, posters everywhere exhorted people to 'carry your gas mask at all times', but there was no apparent danger and no food shortages either. Newspapers carried advertisements for whisky, meat, radios and furniture, and there were plenty of fresh vegetables. Potatoes were selling for one penny per pound and cauliflowers at twopence each. There were plenty of oranges at threepence each.

There was also plenty to grumble about. Everyone had braced themselves for the aerial bombing of innocent civilians, but the last few months of 1939 were an anti-climax. Many people's attitude was, 'We'll face up to whatever Hitler might throw at us, but there is no danger and all we can see is a lot of tiresome, petty regulations.'

One restriction that affected everybody was the blackout. Total blackout was the order and the cry of 'Put that light out!' had people hastily checking their own arrangements in case a small chink of light had escaped into an inky night. Magistrates threatened to get tough with so-called 'lighting offenders' as dozens of otherwise law-abiding citizens found themselves hauled before the courts. Getting about in the blackout was a serious problem. Street lamps were switched off and torches were in short supply. People fumbled about in the dark, apologising to lampposts and pillar-boxes. Fatal road accidents doubled in the last four months of 1939 and the comment was made, more than once, that Hitler appeared to be killing his enemies without the need for air-raids. He just persuaded them to turn off all the lights.

Mea Allan, the *Daily Herald* journalist who would become the first female war correspondent to be permanently accredited to the British Forces and the first female news editor in Fleet Street, felt that the universal blackout was 'a fearful portent of what war would be. We had not thought that we would have to fight in darkness, or that light would be our enemy'. Allan also interviewed Jack the Crumpet Man who, after eighteen years cheerily selling crumpets in London's West End, with his green baize apron, his bell and his tray upon his head, was having to put them all away. 'They won't let me ring me bell anymore,' he told Allan, wistfully, "cos they'd think I was an air-raid.'

The issue of gas masks was another irritation that people accepted, although a spot check revealed that many people used the containers to carry their lunchtime sandwiches. The absence of bombing saw the return of many children who had been evacuated. Parents missed their offspring, the kids were homesick and there was no sign of danger. It seemed a pointless heartache. It was thought that many back home at the beginning of the Christmas holidays might not return to their evacuation areas.

Despite the lack of any land engagement with the enemy, some men became the object of their neighbours' scorn when they refused to be called-up for military service. As the list of reserved occupations was continually modified and more and more men became eligible for call-up, so the number of conscientious objectors grew. Tribunals were set up to deal with their cases, although the number of hearings reported in the early months of the war indicated that there was little consistency in their verdicts. Sometimes a man was deemed a genuine objector, sometimes not. Often their circumstances were the same. One young man in Derby hit upon the idea of ingesting large quantities of scalding hot tea with bread and dripping immediately before his army medical. His hopes that this would somehow render him unfit for military service were soon dashed and so he then became a conscientious objector on religious grounds, which did work. In 1940, tribunals would continue to sit regularly.

The war did not appear to be breaking down social barriers. When Douglas Albert Townsend Smith, a 24-year-old commercial traveller, lost his job because of the war, he started work as a bus conductor. His sweetheart was Diana Vaughan Lucas, the 20-year-old daughter of a Bristol doctor, who he had met while they were both working at an ARP depot. They planned to marry in 1940. However, in the words of Miss Lucas:

'My mother does not approve of my choice because we are not of the same social standing. But all I know is that I love him and will marry him even if I have to wait just over a year until I am 21. I have been told that now I have been made a ward of Chancery there are penalties which go to the length of imprisonment unless we separate, but I would rather go to prison than give him up.'

The pair wanted to appeal to the Chancery Court but before counsel could be briefed, Mr Smith had to find a deposit of £50. He said, 'I am starting work as a bus conductor because I am prepared to do anything rather than wait for something to turn up. I have another job in view but I am going to do the first job available.' There is no record to be found that they ever tied the knot.

As the first Christmas of the war approached, there came news of the first major naval engagement of the conflict. The German pocket battleship *Admiral Graf Spee* had been at sea since the start of the war, sinking several merchant ships but taking all of their crews on board first. In December, three Royal Navy ships, the heavy cruiser HMS *Exeter* and the light cruisers HMS *Ajax* and HMS *Achilles*, closed in on her off the River Plate in Uruguay. The *Exeter* was badly damaged and made for the Falklands, and the *Ajax* was also hit before Captain Hans Langsdorff took the German ship to Montevideo. According to international law, a warship could remain in a neutral port only for twenty-four hours. The *Admiral Graf Spee*, now trapped, remained for seventy-two hours before Langsdorff gave the order to scuttle her. In South Shields, the wife of William Ray, chief engineer of the Blue Star liner *Doric Star*, who had been released from the *Admiral Graf Spee*, received a letter from her husband:

'We had quite a hectic time for twelve days and quite enough excitement to go on with. During the battle we had a hot time and you can imagine our mixed feelings, wanting our own people to win, and yet hoping they would not make too good a job of it. We were lucky that none of our people on board was injured while many of our captors were killed.'

Mr Ray said that they were quite well treated on board the *Admiral Graf Spee* 'although our food consisted mainly of black bread'.

Back home, shops became busier and in many ways it seemed like any pre-war Christmas. Shops offered 'a good selection of toys'. Several suggested gas-mask containers in their guide to last-minute present buying. Opticians advertised Polaroid spectacles for motorists, while Joe Simpson's pawnshop in Derby offered 'highest prices paid' for false teeth.

Cinemas, which had re-opened in September after being closed for a few days while the government decided on its policy concerning places of entertainment, stayed open on Christmas Day and there were queues outside many. The *Birmingham Mail* reported that at the city's Forum cinema there was a mixed fare ranging from 'a war picture with British brains outwitting the enemy spy upon our secrets ... the ultimate overthrow of nefarious machinations, to a comedy in which love triumphs over all'. Hotels were booked to capacity. Local families opened their front doors to servicemen stationed far from their own homes. At the nation's railway stations there were warm embraces as some troops left, their leave over; and joyful reunions as others arrived, their break from duty about to begin.

On the wireless King George VI gave his famous Christmas Day message, 'I said to the man who stood at the gate of the year...' while a NAAFI concert featured Gracie Fields from 'somewhere in France'. Lord Strabogli, speaking for Labour, told the House of Lords that 'people require heartening and their complaint is that the BBC programmes are very depressing'. The *Daily Herald* agreed. 'It still hires, monotonously, the same few artists, night after night.'

Meanwhile, somewhere in England was Una Roe, who had given up her dance studio in the Midlands to go on the stage with Tex Osborne, a cowboy rope expert. Una played the piano accordion while Tex spun his rope. At Christmas 1939 their act, entitled Tex and Una, of course, was entertaining troops at an unnamed barracks.

On Christmas morning in Liverpool, the League of Welldoers distributed 250 hotpots and 250 grocery parcels to needy families and on Boxing Day 'the usual Christmas dinner was provided for ragpickers and sandwichmen and an enjoyable entertainment was given by Madame Olive Lloyd and friends'. In Newcastle, there was a choice of four pantomimes including *Robinson Crusoe*, which had 'a rousing first night' at the Theatre Royal where Man Friday 'stepped out of character to play tunes on a xylophone of jam jars'.

During the Christmas period, a new postal record of more than one million letters had been dealt with in Exeter. On 23 December alone a record number of 800 telegrams had been delivered in the city, while rail traffic in the south-west of England had been fully maintained despite the war and the dreadful weather. Thus, the minutiae of life in wartime Britain carried on. As the *Derby Evening Telegraph* of 27 December 1939 put it, 'It is hard to realise that there is a war on.'

In 1940, Britain would discover that life was going to be different after all.

Chapter One

January 1940

'Disraeli once said that the real motto of the English people is –
"Something will turn up."'

Advertisement for public houses,
The Times, 10 January 1940

On 1 January 1940, the *Manchester Evening News* had a sobering message
for its readers:

'The British Peoples face the year 1940. For the second time within
a quarter of a century they greet the New Year a nation standing
newly at arms. They believe with all the faith and fervour they can
command that it is a just war. History may censure but it cannot
deny the efforts they made to escape it. But now they are committed
… They are confident they will prevail.'

The newspaper pointed out that since the first Sunday in September
1939, in small ways there had been 'a subtle and dangerous change' in
people's outlook. Having prepared themselves for imminent death and
destruction, having sent their children away to comparative safety and
having taken up 'civilian defensive dispositions', they had found that
nothing had happened. There was, said the paper, the growing danger
that the British would be lulled into the delusion of a 'comfortable war'.

Of course, generally speaking, twenty-four hours make no difference
and on New Year's Day 1940 the Second World War looked exactly as it
had on New Year's Eve 1939. And here was the danger; a new year, with
all its good intentions and resolutions and fresh starts, lay ahead. Were
people ready for what it might bring? Or were they still thinking that
this would be a 'comfortable war'? Although the evacuation of children
had not altogether broken down, the percentage of returning evacuees

was alarming. The blackout was nowhere near efficient enough and the number of motorists who conformed to the lighting regulations was overwhelmingly outnumbered by those who did not, while the 'foolish cry' that food rationing was unnecessary and the country could get through without it, was 'a further sign of the failure to appreciate what modern war really means'.

The article neatly summed up how most people felt. Throughout Britain there were the same tiresome, inconvenient restrictions but no real cause for alarm. Look what happened on New Year's Day in the Portsmouth area. People living as far apart as Alverstoke and Cosham, a distance of about 12 miles, described being awakened by 'a long hoot followed by several toots'. Families that had retired for the night went down to their shelters. But there was no air-raid. The authorities said that it might have been a ship passing through Spithead. The *Portsmouth Evening News* reported that although for the most part the New Year had been ushered in without any sign of demonstration – wartime restrictions prohibited the general sounding of sirens, whistles and hooters, and the ringing of church bells – 'some of the more sprightly spirits avoided the strict letter of the regulations by a generous use of motor horns'. Perhaps it was this that had roused residents from their warm beds and sent them hurrying to their cold, damp, draughty shelters. Either way it was yet another false alarm.

In Cheltenham, sirens sounded at 1pm on New Year's Day but the warning and all-clear were given within two minutes of each other. The system was simply being tested and the *Gloucestershire Echo* said that 'no concern was shown by people in the streets ...' A test carried out in Plymouth on New Year's Day had mixed results. According to the *Western Morning News*, in certain parts of the city the wail had been loud enough to waken even the soundest sleepers, but in others it was scarcely audible and, had prior notice not been given, then it 'would have caused no more notice than the wind in the trees'. The chief constable of East Sussex gave notice that a test of the air-raid warning system would be carried out at 10am on the following Saturday, 6 January, but that if an actual air-raid warning was received before then, then the test would not be carried out. Off the Norfolk coast, north of Sheringham, bright flares had been reported but a lifeboat found nothing. Reports that the sound of aircraft off the East Coast had caused an air-raid alarm to be sounded were 'without foundation. No air-raid warning was given'.

There had been some action. The Air Ministry announced that an aircraft of Coastal Command had shot down a German aircraft over the North Sea, while anti-aircraft guns had opened fire over the Shetland Islands and there were reports of two German aircraft dropping bombs, but within 45 minutes the all-clear sounded. The only casualties were three sheep that could be added to the unfortunate rabbit killed on an earlier raid on the islands. Almost everywhere, though, as a new year dawned, everyone got on with whatever it was they were doing.

On the political front, there was a surprise on 5 January at the dismissal, only four months into the war, of the Secretary of State for War, Leslie Hore-Belisha, in favour of Oliver Stanley, the son of the Earl of Derby. The business occupied Fleet Street for days and the public were treated to almost a running commentary. There had been friction between the War Office and Hore-Belisha, who had expressed a lack of confidence in the commander-in-chief of the British Expeditionary Force (BEF) in France, Lord Gort. Neville Chamberlain, believed that this was impeding the development of a war that, ironically, Hore-Belisha wanted to prosecute with great vigour. For his part, Hore-Belisha believed that Gort – Hore-Belisha it was who had appointed him in the first place – and his chief-of-staff, General Henry Pownall, simply were not up to the job. In turn they resented the way that he made important decisions without consulting them, including high-level appointments and even doubling the size of the Territorial Army. Sir Oswald Mosley, leader of the British Union of Fascists, had described Hore-Belisha as a 'Jewish warmonger' and anti-Semitism certainly seemed to have been an issue. In his diary, Pownall said:

> 'The ultimate fact is that they could never get on – you couldn't expect two such utterly different people to do so – a great gentleman and an obscure, shallow-brained, charlatan, political Jewboy.'

The reality was that although his opponents were his military subordinates, they still wielded enough influence and power to win the day. In the *Daily Herald*, Hannen Swaffer declared that 'the Brass Hats have won ... influence has successfully pulled the strings and got rid of someone too much in the limelight'. Gort, said Swaffer, had humanised the Army:

'... making the soldier's life a much more happy one, giving non-coms more of a chance of promotion ... Leslie rushed around the camps ... his smile cheered up the soldiers ... "Things are going splendidly," said everyone ... Then Neville started a Blitzkrieg of his own. He annihilated his Secretary of State for War! Now what on earth has been going on behind the scenes? Whom did Leslie offend? What did he refuse to do?'

Hore-Belisha had enjoyed popularity with ordinary soldiers and ordinary civilians, too. Newspapers up and down the country took issue. The *Birmingham Gazette* said that the public was entitled to expect the House of Commons 'to probe the matter deeper for general enlightenment'. The *Nottingham Journal* felt that the prime minister 'must be prepared to receive only half-satisfied approval for his rather half-hearted reshufflement'. The *Western Daily Press* said that the country 'will await with some impatience the explanation of an event which, on the available evidence, is beyond comprehension'. The Manchester-based *Daily Dispatch* declared that 'the nation will receive the news with mixed emotions'. Whatever the explanation, four months later Stanley, too, would be out of the job, replaced in the new Churchill government by Anthony Eden.

If people wondered why Hore-Belisha had been sacked, one fact that no one needed telling was that 1940 had got off to an unusually cold start, although it was some time before the extreme weather could be officially reported. The *Sunday Pictorial* of 28 January explained:

'The weather we have here may spread to Germany and so, in order to avoid presenting Adolf Hitler with a ready-made weather forecast, we do not print news of the weather for at least fifteen days after it happened.'

The people of Ambleside in particular were fully aware that records were being broken. The bitterly cold weather had begun three days before

Christmas and on 21 January, the temperature in the Westmoreland town dipped to minus 21 degrees Centigrade. It was a full week later, however, before newspapers mentioned how cold it was at the start of the year. Even then the situation in Ambleside seven days earlier was still a closely guarded secret

Under the banner headline 'We Couldn't Tell You This Before!' the *Sunday Pictorial* revealed that in the first two weeks of the month the 'Thames was frozen from bank to bank for miles ... Barges were locked in ice for days – even steamers couldn't move ... Bursting house boilers killed dozens; injured hundreds ... There were 28 degrees of frost for days'. It was, said the paper, Britain's coldest weather for 125 years. This was not true but the month was certainly the country's second-coldest January of the twentieth century, the Thames had indeed frozen up for the first time in six decades and when mild air from the south-west met cold air from the north-east it produced heavy snowfalls that saw Sheffield under 4ft of the white stuff. Where rain fell instead of snow, trees, telegraph wires and power lines were coated in ice so thick that it brought down branches and disrupted communications and the electricity supply. It was the longest lasting 'ice storm' – 27 January to 3 February 1940 – ever recorded in Britain's history.

On Monday, 29 January, the *Daily Herald* reported on the 'Greatest Rail Hold-up Ever'. The newspaper told readers:

'Delays and dislocations on the railways of Britain this weekend were the worst in living memory. Last night trains were arriving in London from Scotland more than twelve hours behind time. Mainline communication between Yorkshire and Lancashire was severed. Three trains were "lost" in Scotland. Hold-up of food supplies was feared in the North.'

The *Scottish Royal Mail* that had left Aberdeen at 3pm on Saturday finally arrived at Euston at 5.10pm the following day. A member of the train crew told of their journey. 'We were held up at one place for three hours. At another we covered 100 yards in an hour.' It had been daybreak when most of the passengers learned that their train was far behind time. After a fitful night's sleep they had got up, washed and dressed and readied themselves to alight at Euston, only to discover that they had not yet arrived at Preston. The east-west line was blocked between Guide Bridge and Penistone and although relays of workmen, reinforced by parties of soldiers, had worked non-stop throughout the night, there was small hope of that the line would be reopened that day.

Meanwhile, 75 per cent of passenger services in and out of Manchester were cancelled and trains on services to Brighton, Hastings, Guildford, Reading, Ascot and Portsmouth were running up to six hours behind schedule. Mr F.H. Chapman of Twickenham told of his journey to Waterloo – less than 12 miles – that had taken two hours:

> 'First we had to wait three-quarters of an hour for our train. When one arrived, the first 2 miles took half an hour. At times it would not have been difficult to walk faster than the train was going. On one slight incline we people watching from windows invited each other to come out and give the train a push.'

Hundreds of soldiers returning from leave would not reach their barracks in time, and in 'one place in Scotland' a parcel completed its ten-mile journey by rowing boat after the train carrying it became stuck. One train carrying Bud Flanagan, Chesney Allen, Jimmy Nervo and Teddy Knox, all members of the Crazy Gang, the zany bunch of comedians that had been delighting theatre audiences since the early 1930s, had left London at 11pm, on their way to a charity concert in aid of the British Red Cross and not arrived at Brighton until 5.40am. 'The comedians gave their fellow passengers the longest show they had ever done,' reported the *Daily Herald*. Ironically, that week British cinemas were showing a film starring the Crazy Gang, entitled *Frozen Limits*, a comedy set in Alaska. Members of Henry Hall's dance band were injured when the coach in which they were travelling back to London from Bristol hit a street light standard during the blackout in an icy Reading. Henry Hall himself was shaken but unhurt, but Freddie Mann, Ted Farrar and Roy Copestake were badly cut by flying glass.

In one street in Birmingham, snow brought the roofs of thirty houses crashing in. Neighbours ran to help the occupants remove their furniture, which was placed in Birmingham Corporation lorries and carried to municipal flats. But roofs kept falling at intervals and several helpers had to run back home when their own properties began to collapse. In Brixton, one house was completely ruined when a burst water pipe resulted in ceilings collapsing storey by storey until they all arrived on the ground floor. Meanwhile, George VI went skating on the Royal Lake in the grounds of Windsor Castle 'and in another part of the country, Princess Elizabeth and Princess Margaret were on the ice almost daily'.

In Suffolk, mail had to be delivered on horseback because 4ft-deep snowdrifts blocked country roads and East Anglian farmers in general were facing disastrous times. In the first half of January, milk yield had fallen by half and egg production by more than a third as thousands of birds were found frozen to death. The Ipswich to London road was impassable to motorists for days and in South Cambridgeshire, 30 degrees of frost was recorded.

In Kent, blizzard followed blizzard, forming snowdrifts 14ft deep in parts. No vehicular traffic could leave Deal, pits were idle as coal miners could not get to work, and icicles hung from the rigging of ships trapped in harbour. Fires had to be lit under steam winches before anchors could be moved and in part of Folkestone harbour, the sea froze. At nearby Capel-le-Ferne, perched on the White Cliffs of Dover, the whole village was without paraffin and a youth reportedly walked 15 miles to obtain one gallon. There was worse to come than bad weather, though. Today, Capel-le-Ferne is home to a memorial to the pilots of the Battle of Britain that, before 1940 was out, would be fought in the skies above the village.

On Dartmoor, ponies were found frozen to death after blizzards swept the West Country. Fourteen degrees of frost were recorded in Exeter and the River Exe was frozen over from its source on Exmoor to a point only ten miles from its mouth. On some farms frost had penetrated fields to a depth of 2ft. In Brecon, long queues of people carrying buckets and jugs formed in order to collect water from the fortunate few whose pipes had not frozen up. Nearly the whole town was deprived of its supply, despite being only a few miles from giant reservoirs at Cardiff and Swansea. Fast flowing Welsh rivers that had never been known to freeze for half a century were ice-covered. In rural parts of the Principality, people were forced to melt snow to make a pot of tea and then spoon out milk that had frozen in the bottle.

Whether, as the *Sunday Pictorial* claimed, bursting boilers had killed dozens of people in January 1940, the cold weather was blamed for the deaths of six members of one Newcastle family when their house boiler exploded in the St Anthony's district of the city that month. Twenty-nine-year-old Charles Sharp, his sons Charles Jameson (who was almost 5) and John Thomas (1) and 10-year-old Iris Vincent, the father's sister-in-law, were killed outright. Two-year-old Iris Sharp and her mother, Winfred Sharp (25), died later in hospital. Newcastle's city architect, Mr R.G. Roberts, issued a warning. 'If tenants find they are unable to obtain water from the hot tap then they should immediately draw the fire and turn off the main stop tap to the house.' The lord mayor, Councillor A.D. Russell, also visited the house and gave a warning against allowing fire to heat boilers when the water tank had run dry. 'I can only express the hope that the public will take heed of the warning this appalling tragedy gives to the city.'

Although newspapers were forbidden to publish details of the weather until much later, for fear of providing the enemy with a weather forecast, it is doubtful that Hitler did not already know that it was more than just nippy. A centre of cold stretched from Amsterdam through Bremen, Hamburg and Berlin – which was experiencing its coldest winter for 110 years – to Königsberg. Because of heavily frozen seas and rivers, many German naval vessels could not be moved for a considerable time. In Britain, the general public were aware of this. Unlike the weather in their own country, they had only to pick up a newspaper to see how cold it was in Germany. There were 200 tankers and 400 grain ships bound for German ports but stuck in the frozen Danube. In fact, when it came to the bad weather that the Axis was also enduring, it was even snowing in Rome.

For many, however, the weather was the least of their concerns. On 1 January, a Royal Proclamation had been published requiring five further age classes to register under the National Service Armed Forces Act. The new registration raised the age limit from 23 to 28, the object of which was to increase the figure of 1.5 million already under arms or waiting to be called up – not counting those provided by the Dominions, the Indian Empire and the colonies – to 2.5 million. The *Dundee Courier* commented:

'... both at home and abroad the effect of the step taken will be psychologically important. It emphasises in the mind of both friend and enemy the complete unreserve with which Britain means to use her power in the prosecution of the war'.

The *Daily Herald* told the story of 23-year-old general clerk Ernest Steele who was one of 250,000 men in his age category who were awaiting call-up. Ernest worked at a builder's merchants in Paddington where he earned a weekly wage of £2 10s, of which he gave his mother £1 plus an extra 2s now that the war had increased the cost of living. He cycled to work every morning, arriving at 8.30am and leaving at 5.30pm. He took his lunch in a bag and joined three other young clerks in eating together, in summer on the grass in Hyde Park, in winter at a coffee stall just around the corner. Since the war began he had been moved around constantly – he was now working in his eighth department – to supplement depleted staffing levels. The *Herald* said:

'The greatest change, however, is always that sense of impermanence, since conscription impends. It does not scare him, or affect him much in any way, but it is simply always there ... He really wishes that it would happen soon. Waiting cannot help but be irksome.'

Ernest's life, at work and outside of work, said the newspaper, was so ordinary, so prosaic:

'It looks as if it might go on for ever, monotonous, a little dreary, a little unimportant. And there, just beyond the counter, lie trenches, khaki, tanks, guns, possibly death.'

Meanwhile, the authorities had other problems. On New Year's Day, 100,000 volunteers were still needed to give blood. Lady Constance Malleson of Blagdon in Somerset wrote to the *Western Daily Press*:

'... Am I not fairly correct in saying (on a rough reckoning) that if one-third of the Bristol population volunteered, the appeal of the Army Blood Supply Depot in Bristol would be met? At the risk of appearing ungracious to British women, I would point out that in Finland such an appeal would not be necessary. There women volunteers – of every class – under military orders prepared to render whatever service need whenever needed ... I can think of no better New Year resolution for all fit people than to present themselves as soon as possible at one of Bristol's leading hospitals for a blood test.'

The war headlines told of the new rules and regulations that affected most people, but there were also vivid reminders that elsewhere there really was a war going on. On 9 January, in the North Sea, three small unescorted merchant ships – two Danish and one British – were attacked by German aircraft, but the main headline of the day was reserved for the fate of the Union Castle line's 10,000-ton passenger ship *Dunbar Castle*. Part of a convoy en route to South Africa, she had activated a magnetic mine between the North Foreland and Ramsgate. The *Dunbar Castle*, which had just left Southend, broke her back and sank rapidly on an even keel in shallow water with the loss of nine lives, including that of her master, Captain Henry Causton, who was killed when a section of mast fell on to the ship's bridge. The tragedy could have been far greater. The trawler *Calvi* rescued 189 passengers and crew. For days after the sinking, the shore was littered with debris that included boxes of pencils and even a grand piano.

On 16 January, around 150 families received mixed news of their loved ones serving in the Royal Navy. That day the Admiralty announced the loss of three submarines in the Heligoland Bight. The crews of HMS *Starfish* and HMS *Undine* had been taken prisoner but HMS *Seahorse* had failed to return to port in Blyth and her fate remained a mystery. It was later learned that the *Seahorse* had also been sunk, in her case with the loss of her entire 39-man crew.

There were fatalities much closer to home and people were now becoming jittery about the causes. On 19 January, five workers were killed when an explosion in a nitro-glycerine drying shed at the Royal Gunpowder Factory at Waltham Abbey in Essex was heard twenty miles away. The Press Association reported that in addition to the five men who died, thirty workers were injured. One worker told a reporter:

'I was about 100 yards away from the shed, I saw a blinding flash
and there was a terrific explosion. I was thrown on to my back and
before I could get up there was another explosion.'

Newspapers suggested that a saboteur might be to blame but after its
detectives had investigated the blast Scotland Yard assured the public
that 'there is no reason to suspect that the explosions were caused by
sabotage'.

Nonetheless, rumours continued to abound in the increasingly
uneasy atmosphere of war and there was a public outcry when, under
headlines such as 'Friend Of Hitler Comes Home' and '"Pure Aryan"
Comes Home', newspapers reported the arrival back in Britain of Unity
Mitford, one of the six daughters of Lord Redesdale, whose sister, Diana,
had married Sir Oswald Mosley. Unity Mitford had spent several years
in Nazi Germany and was huge admirer of Hitler. It was rumoured that
she had had a sexual relationship with the Fuhrer. Whatever the truth of
that, when Britain declared war a distraught Unity went to the *Englischer
Garten* park in Munich and shot herself in the head. With a bullet lodged
in her brain, the now disabled former socialite arrived at Folkestone on
3 January, an event that was widely reported. Patrick Dollan, the lord
provost of Glasgow, spoke for many when he said, 'It is simply disgusting
that this attention should have been paid to a little flapper who really
ought to have her pants smacked instead of getting publicity.'

Under its 'What We Think' column, the *Manchester Evening News*
made no bones about it:

'Miss Unity Mitford is home. Let her stay there. The fuss that has
been made over this young woman – armed guards, fixed bayonets
and whatnot – is absurd. There is a war on, and she is of no
consequence to it. There are plenty of other people worth guarding
– and talking about.'

The *Daily Herald* agreed:

'The return of Hitler's friend was turned into a screaming joke.
Masses of marching police, and the might of the Navy, the Army

and the Air Force – yes, even a Blackpool coastguard band – were shown arrayed, either to protect, or to glorify, a silly girl.'

George Ward Price, who got to know Hitler and his entourage well while working as a foreign correspondent for the *Daily Mail* – in his 1937 book *I Know These Dictators* he described Hitler as having 'a pleasant, human personality … a fondness for children and dogs …' – thought differently:

> 'There was never any doubt about her personal influence with the Fuhrer, though I never believed it extended to his political activities … It is pity rather than blame that Unity Mitford deserves as she returns to her own country.'

Her family issued a statement to the effect that Unity Mitford did not know that there was a war on. 'She does not appreciate what has happened.' On 24 January, however, it was still a topic engaging parliament. In the House of Commons, Herbert Morrison, the Labour MP for Hackney South who in October would become Winston Churchill's home secretary, asked the prime minister:

> 'What steps were taken by, or on behalf of His Majesty's Government to facilitate the return of Miss Unity Mitford to this country; and on whose authority was both military and police protection provided for her at the port of arrival?'

Neville Chamberlain replied:

> 'No steps were taken by the Government in connection with this case other than those which are taken in ordinary circumstances for other British subjects … The only action taken by the Foreign Office on Miss Mitford's behalf was the inclusion of her name in a list of British subjects in Germany for whom the United States Embassy were requested to do whatever might be possible, and the sending of a telegraphic inquiry about her health through the agency of the United States Embassy. Such inquiries have been made in respect of British subjects on several occasions when they have appeared to be justified by the urgency of the case.'

Mr Morrison was not satisfied:

'As it is now apparent that His Majesty's Government did take steps, may I ask the prime minister why he did not tell me so in the first instance? May I also ask him why the Government should take steps to facilitate the return of a British subject who would be much better occupied in continuing the activities she was engaged on in assisting an enemy government? Finally, will the Right Honourable Gentleman tell me what would have been done if this had been a working-class person?'

Mavis Tate, the Conservative MP for Frome, wanted to know, 'May I ask the Right Honourable Gentleman whether he is prepared to support the expulsion from this country of Communists because they are helping an enemy government?' There was no reply.

Unity Mitford would die in 1948 in Oban at the age of 33 as a result of meningitis caused by swelling around the bullet lodged in her brain. One year earlier, Mavis Tate had taken her own life by gassing herself at her home in Pimlico.

On New Year's Day 1940, the second batch of Canadian troops to arrive in Britain since the beginning of the war landed as a 'west coast port'. Artillery drawn from Winnipeg and Montreal, engineers from Toronto and Halifax, signal and service corps units and infantry that included several kilted Scottish regiments accompanied by their own pipe band were officially welcomed by Anthony Eden, the dominions secretary, who said:

'Together with those who preceded you a few weeks ago, you form the active service force that Canada has sent to fight by our side with those of the other members of the British Commonwealth and of our allies in a common cause. A nation from the New World is offering its help to challenge tyranny in the Old. Your example is a guarantee of final victory, but it is something more than that. It is an inspiration to freedom-loving peoples everywhere.'

In the meantime life in Britain went on. At the Royalty Theatre in Chester, Janette on the rolling globe gave 'an act of beauty and balance', while Jan Dokskanky performed with his cage of forest-bred lions, a group of polar bears, and an elephant act that was 'much appreciated'. The following week there would be Rusty and Shine 'already known to Chester audiences for their sparkling humour', and Kendo and Hanako, 'an Eastern speciality'.

So not all the news was about the war, although the conflict was still being blamed for most things. On 24 January, Coco the Clown appeared at Windsor County Court on judgement summonses of £14. He said that since the war began he had worked variously as a hotel night porter, a labourer digging up roads, a photographer and as a pantomime clown. He had also worked for the Army for two days for 10s. The 39-year-old Coco, whose real name was Nicolai Poliakoff and who lived in Ascot, told the court that the war had hit the circus very hard. Because of the blackout regulations they had gone completely out of business. He promised Judge Digby Cotes-Preedy that he would use the first royalty from the book of his life story, to be published shortly, to discharge the debt. An order for payment of one shilling a month was made. His book was finally published in 1941, by which time the war had taken an even darker turn for Britain.

Chapter Two

Make Do and Mend

'The cry would go up: "Brown's have got some custard creams!"
and whoosh, a queue of kids had formed in seconds.'

Brenda Shaw, Hull

On 8 January 1940, the government introduced food rationing. The newly
established Ministry of Food had already issued every person in Britain
with a ration book and the holders of those books – or, most often, the
housewife on behalf of her entire family – had to register with nominated
retailers. The Ministry explained its reasons for the introduction of
rationing; half the nation's meat and most of its bacon, butter and sugar
came from overseas and it was unreasonable to ask sailors to risk their
lives to bring in unnecessary cargoes. Now more ships would be released
to supply the war effort with vital raw materials. Also, if divided equitably,
then rationing would ensure ample food for over 44 million people. Seven
days before rationing was introduced, the Ministry of Food issued this
advice:

'Do make certain that you have registered with your supplier for
bacon, ham, sugar and butter. If you have left it till now, do it at
once.

'Do use lots of potatoes and as much fish as you can get.

'Do notice that eggs are getting cheaper, and that plenty of home-
produced poultry is now available.

'Do remember that the small discomfort entailed in rationing is
nothing compared with the national service it involves.'

Rationing, the Ministry said, prevented uncertainty and meant that there
would be no need to queue as people did in the First World War when

rationing was not introduced until 1918. But, as shortages increased, so long queues for unrationed goods became commonplace. Word would spread: 'Mr Brown has had a delivery of onions.' And housewives would rush to his shop. Sometimes they joined a queue without knowing what reward would be at the end of it.

At first it was only bacon and ham, butter and sugar that were restricted. At the onset, each person's weekly allowance was 12oz of sugar, 4oz of butter, and 4oz of bacon or ham – you could not have both. Meat was rationed from 11 March 1940 but, unlike all other rationed foodstuffs, allowances were measured by cost not weight. Initially the ration per person per week was 1s 10d worth of meat. This would be reduced to 1s 2d in July 1941 and would remain at that for the rest of the war. From May, cheese (1oz per week) and, from 9 July, tea (2oz per week) were added to the list. The inclusion of tea meant that many workers would now have to use their own precious ration to enjoy a mid-shift break. On 24 July, a sympathetic government announced:

> 'The Ministry of Food has authorised Food Control Committees to issue special permits for industrial, business and clerical workers in cases where they cannot obtain tea from the registered canteens. This will enable them to have tea during working hours without drawing on domestic rations.'

Cooking fats were also rationed in July 1940 and more items would follow in 1941, although bread, potatoes and other vegetables together with fruit, fish and coffee would never be rationed. Children did not receive the tea ration but could have extra fruit juice, and people with special needs, such as diabetics, were catered for. Children and expectant or nursing mothers would be allocated extra milk and eggs. As early as 1937, vegetarians had lobbied the government for recognition but it would be 1942 before they secured more eggs, cheese and nuts in exchange for the meat that they did not claim.

In January 1940, a letter writer to the *Nottingham Evening Post* reminded people:

> 'Turning to a good way of helping our indomitable seafaring men, remember that good slogan "Dig For Victory". Why not dig up half

your lawn for the duration of the war? If everyone who could did that it would make a great contribution to the food production of the nation.'

The slogan had come into official use in October 1939, shortly after the government launched a drive to increase the number of allotments in England and Wales by half a million. In a broadcast to the nation, the Minister of Agriculture, Sir Reginald Dorman-Smith, said, 'Let "Dig For Victory" be the motto of everyone with a garden and of every able-bodied man and woman capable of digging an allotment in their spare time.' In fact the words had first been publicly used at least a fortnight earlier, in a headline in the *Bedfordshire Times and Independent*.

Even before war had begun, the government had produced its 'Food Defence Plans' that allowed for an increased consumption of potatoes, oatmeal, cheese, carrots and green vegetables. Vitamins A and D that occurred naturally in butter would be added to margarine, and extra calcium would be added to 'National Bread'.

The *Daily Express* had always been against food rationing, running what almost amounted to a campaign against its introduction. In January 1940, the paper said that food rationing had only been brought in because a 'vast organisation' was already in being and that rationing simply gave its staff something to do. 'The Ministry of Food employ nearly 11,000 persons. If they were disbanded, we could buy 100,000 cows for the same money.'

Polls taken by Mass Observation and the British Institute of Public Opinion (BIPO) showed that the public did not agree. The BIPO poll showed that 60 per cent of those questioned thought that rationing was necessary; 28 per cent were against it being introduced; 12 per cent said, 'Don't know'. A Liverpool housewife told Mass Observation, 'I wish to goodness they would introduce rationing. At least I would be able to go into a shop and get what I was allowed.'

Far from introducing a job creation scheme, the problem that the government foresaw was that Britain relied heavily on imports for its food, especially meat and fruit. An enemy would obviously target merchant shipping, countries from where some foods came from might be occupied and bombing might destroy warehouses where food was stored. Within a week of the outbreak of war, the Ministry of Food was operational with

Lord Woolton now the nation's Minister of Food. Generally in times of shortages price increases were the most effective form of control, but in these now extreme times that would leave the better-off to eat well and the poor to go hungry. There was a war on. It had to be fair shares all round. The working class would be entitled to the same amounts as the middle class and the rich. In 1940, though, there was already limited choice and availability. While rationing was seen as fair, sometimes it was the inability to buy unrationed goods that caused friction. A customer with limited means might be told, 'Sorry, we're out of stock.' But when a 'best customer' asked for the same, the item would miraculously appear from under the counter or from 'out the back'.

There were some spectacular examples. In March 1940 Mrs Yvonne Reekie of Bovingdon in Hertfordshire was fined £50 for obtaining sugar – equivalent to the weekly ration for 140 people – in excess of the amount prescribed in the Rationing Order and £25 for obtaining it without a coupon, from John Kay Ltd in Watford. A summons against the shop for supplying the sugar was adjourned. The court was told that on 24 February, an employee of the Food Control Committee saw a Rolls-Royce drive up to Kay's shop. A chauffeur was seen leaving the shop carrying a large cardboard box that contained blue bags. The box was placed in the car and it was driven away with Mrs Reekie inside.

'I admit the whole thing,' said Mrs Reekie. 'I paid Kay's manager two guineas. I did not get a receipt. Why should one shop have so much sugar by them and so tempt people? I realise that what I did was wrong but, at the same time, I was only doing what any housewife would have done.' Not many housewives did their shopping by chauffeur-driven Rolls-Royce.

If anyone could afford to dine out elsewhere, then those meals were 'off-ration' – and expensive. West End restaurants continued to enjoy patronage from rich customers. It did not go down well. On 8 July 1940, Lord Woolton broadcast to the nation:

> 'I have told you already that when restrictions are necessary I shall impose them without hesitation and without apology. I am stopping luxurious feeding and I have arranged for the consumption of food in hotels and restaurants to be reduced.'

The introduction, in 1942, of a five-shilling top limit on what could be charged for a meal finally put an end to the most ostentatious – many felt unseemly – examples. There were, though, many restaurants, cafes and teashops that continued to provide the occasional and sensibly priced treat. For working people, 'British Restaurants' that were run by local authorities in premises as diverse as church halls, schools and empty shops, offered a three-course lunch for only ninepence. The scheme had grown out of London County Council's Londoners' Meals Service introduced in September 1940 during the Blitz.

Meanwhile, on Monday, 1 April 1940, *The Scotsman* reported a 'whisky famine in Glasgow'. The paper said that after several Glasgow pubs had exhausted their supply on the Saturday evening, 'customers were compelled to take other forms of refreshment'. Was it an All Fools' Day jape? It sounded not. Would a Scotsman joke about such a thing? The Scottish Licensed Trade Defence Association was going to approach the Customs and Excise Department to complain about restrictions of issues from bonded warehouses. If more supplies were not forthcoming than a reduction in licensing hours might have to be applied.

On 23 April 1940, the Chancellor of the Exchequer, Sir John Simon, announced his budget. The government was looking to raise an all-time record of £1.234 billion to finance the war to March 1941. The new burdens on British taxpayers were:

Beer – an increase of 1d a pint.

Spirits – additional tax of 1s 9d a bottle, bringing the retail price of whisky to 16s a bottle.

Tobacco – increase equivalent to 3d per ounce. Cigarettes at present costing 7d for a packet of 10 would now cost another 8.5d

Matches – a box of 50 matches would now cost 1.5d, up from 1d. They would raise £4 million in a full year.

Letter Post – cost per 2oz would now be 2.5d, up from 1.5d.

Telephone charges would increase by 15 per cent on everything including calls and line rental.

Telegrams would now cost 9d for nine words, up from 6d.

A new tax – purchase tax – would affect sales of goods other than raw materials for industry, food, drink, gas and electricity, and articles already heavily taxed, such as alcohol, tobacco and petrol.

Income tax would now be 7s 6d in the £.

Surtax would now be charged on incomes over £1,500 per annum. Previously the starting point was £2,000.

Bonus shares were now prohibited, and dividends paid by public companies would be limited.

The Chancellor explained to the House of Commons:

> 'I come to increased charge on the smaller incomes – what somebody has called the £5 to £12-a-week man. I extract two or three litigations … such as in the case of a married man with children. If he earns £300 a year he will pay £15 [per year] in Income Tax instead of the £7 he paid last year, and £5 the year before. If he earns £400 a year he will pay £30 12s 6d this year instead of £17 10s last year, and £12 12s 6d the year before. If he earns £600 a year he will pay £92, 16s 3d instead of £73 10s last year and £60 the year before.'

Sir John estimated that in the current year this would raise £42.5 million, and in a full year £61.75 million.

Labour MPs generally shared the view of Conservative members, that the proposed purchase tax would be far too complicated ever to reach the Statute Book in anything like the form proposed by the Chancellor. According to the Press Association's lobby correspondent, it would have to be abandoned or drastically modified, or replaced by a more easily understood sales tax, or a stamp duty on all articles – except those already exempt – sold in shops. In fact, Purchase Tax was introduced in October 1940.

In an attempt to gauge public opinion on matters of more interest to the working man, the *Newcastle Evening Chronicle* sent a reporter to talk to local people. Curiously, five of the six tobacconist shops they visited reported no rush to buy extra cigarettes, but a stampede to stock up on matches. One shop had sold out.

An office caretaker said, 'What I don't like is the new postage. I have three lads in the Army and all in England. I write to them regularly … I will have to cut my letters down, and so will my lads. I generally send them a few stamps when I write, but I can't afford to do that now.'

A soldier said that he could not get on with smoking a pipe. 'I've tried over and over again. I'm going on to gaspers at ten for a tanner [6d]. They are a smaller smoke, but a smoke.'

A sailor commented, 'I'm not worrying. I'm hardly ever at home and we get our baccy cheap enough.'

A businessman said, 'I've always smoked a good class cigarette, and will continue to do so but I am cutting them down. I travelled in a non-smoker this morning, for the first time in years. That saved a couple.'

A builder's labourer thought that 'the beer tax is not as bad as I expected. I'm going to cut out a lot of baccy.' An unemployed labourer told the reporter, 'I haven't much baccy now. I'll just have to do with less.'

Most licensees in Leeds told a *Yorkshire Evening Post* reporter that the 1s 9d increase on a bottle would result in a reduction in whisky drinking. The demand for the spirit before the Budget had been brisk. The *Aberdeen Press and Journal* called it 'a grim, tax-everything-but-food budget'. The paper said:

'Everyman's luxuries – such as beer, spirits and tobacco – and even his necessities – such as matches, postage stamps, telephone calls and telegrams – will cost him more as a result of the second war Budget, while his income will be more severely taxed than ever.'

Yet the paper also found it 'a realistic budget':

'Sir John Simon's first wholesale wartime Budget is not like so depressing as some people imagined it would be … it seeks to find money where money is made, or where money is spent in large amounts on commodities which are not, in the ultimate sense, absolutely essential.'

Petrol had been rationed since 22 September 1939 but most people did not own a motor vehicle. Only when it was decided to ban pleasure motoring was there an outcry, not just from the middle and upper classes who could afford a car but also from shopkeepers and guesthouse proprietors who relied on day-trippers for a living.

On 18 June 1940, the issue of 'joyriding' was raised in in the House of Commons after Geoffrey Lloyd, the Conservative MP for Birmingham Ladywood and the minister in charge of the Petroleum Warfare Department, told members:

> 'The House will be glad to know that, as a result of action taken by the Government before and since the war, our supplies of petrol are at present very satisfactory. Substantial economies in the civil consumption of petrol have already been made by rationing, and this automatically secures a corresponding economy in lubricating oil. I have recently issued a new Rationing Order, designed to check abuses in the use of petrol, and I am proceeding with the appointment of inspectors to aid in this purpose. In view of these facts, I do not propose at this moment to make a further general reduction in petrol allowances, but I would emphasise that it is vital that all petrol users should cooperate to the full in the strict observance of the Rationing Order.'

William Leach (Labour, Bradford Central) asked:

> 'What does the Minister mean by the abuse of petrol? Is joyriding an abuse; is going to a racecourse, in the circumstances of the day, an abuse; is taking your best girl out an abuse? Is the Minister satisfied that he has adequate power at this moment to deal with wasteful expenditure of petrol by private users?'

Mr Lloyd replied:

> 'It is not an abuse to use the limited amount of petrol allowed in the basic ration for purposes of reasonable recreation, but it is an abuse to use petrol given on a supplementary allowance for purposes for which it is not given. In regard to that, I have powers, and I intend to use them. Prosecutions will be taken in proper cases, and I am appointing inspectors for that work.'

Thomas Levy (Conservative, Elland) said:

> 'Is my Honourable Friend aware that a number of manufacturers engaged on national work who are using motor transport find that they have absolutely insufficient to do this work of national importance, and that they still see this colossal amount of joyriding and the wastage of petrol, which ought to be controlled in some manner? If there is ample petrol, give this transport that is used for national service sufficient quantities.'

Mr Lloyd assured him that 'no issue of petrol for domestic purposes in the basic ration in any way prejudices the issue for national purposes'.

On 20 July, the government issued a new Acquisition and Disposal of Motor Vehicle Order so that no one could buy a new car, van or lorry without a licence from the Ministry of Transport. Motorcycles not adapted for carrying goods, tractors and mowing machines were exempt, as were vehicles for export. Dealers voiced the belief that motor manufacturers would still make a good profit from exports, which reassured shareholders. The *Hull Daily Mail* thought that although the ban on anyone in Britain buying a new car might upset the routine of those 'who make a practice of exchanging their vehicles every second year, and even be a hardship to businessmen who have long distances to cover', the needs of the individual were nothing compared to those of the nation. Taylor Brothers of Walsall reminded people that while they could not buy a new car 'you can buy a new cycle – and new you can't buy a better cycle than the Rudge'. You could take away 'Britain's best-selling bicycle' for '10s down'.

On the first day of food rationing, the *Lancashire Evening Post* announced, 'Today will be known as Coupon Monday.' The *Daily Mirror* assured the nation that 'The king, too, is on rations,' and the Windsor food controller said that when the royals were stopping at Windsor Castle their travelling ration cards would come down with all the Royal Household cards.

In advertising their Sugar Coated Blood and Stomach Pills, Parkinsons Ltd of Burnley took up the same theme of national sacrifice that had been promoted by the Ministry of Food. The company reminded people:

'To stand up to long hours at the counter, to cope with ration cards and blackouts, day after day, week after week – this calls for stamina of a high order. No one doing such a real job of national service can afford to neglect inside fitness.'

Apparently, it was claimed, no other laxative was as pleasant to take.

People began to prepare for a long war. The *Derby Evening Telegraph* joined forces with the Derby Gas, Light and Coke Company to arrange a series of lectures entitled 'Economic Wartime Cookery', given by Beryl Abbey at the Temperance Hall in Curzon Street. More advice came from the monthly magazine *Britannia and Eve*, which had news of a gadget for making one's butter ration go twice as far. A 'clean and workmanlike churn' made two pounds of merged butter from a pound of butter and a pint of milk. The butter was cut into slices and put into the churn with the milk. This was then stood in a pan of hot water, then the top screwed on and the mixer brought into action. After the mixture had hardened, 'you will like the result ... sweet, wholesome and nourishing'. The churn cost from 8s to 21s. No clue was given as to what refinements were missing from the cheapest version. The same magazine asked readers how they were helping the morale of the nation. Because of rationing did they go around with a face like Cleopatra's Needle? It suggested that housewives could get together and collect peelings, scraps of bread, bones and so on. 'Perhaps there is a farmer in the country just beyond your suburb who would be willing to call for pig fodder two or three times a week.' In the meantime, 'housewives should form their menus from whatever happens to be flush on the market at the time of shopping. Don't grumble if one particular thing is unobtainable ... Explore every economic possibility ...'

In July, the nation's timber controller, Major A.I. Harris, hinted that women might not mind sacrificing the fashion of high heels for the sake of saving precious wood. Major Harris said:

'Supplies from Europe are now cut off from us, but we are shipping now a larger quantity of timber than we have shipped since the war began. Economy is none the less important. With less essential articles there will be all the economy possible. Perhaps women will not mind giving up their high heels for the sake of this economy. Some of these are three and a half inches high. They represent thousands of tons of shipping space.'

Other economies being investigated by a committee including timber being used for furniture, wireless sets, sports goods, clogs and ice-cream spoons.

In the meantime, there were other personal matters to consider, and cosmetics were something not on ration. In 1940, a book entitled *Technique For Beauty* told the women of Britain, 'The stress and strain of war can easily make you lose interest in your personal appearance. But it is up to you to take care of yourself for the sake of other people.' There were also practical considerations. For instance, Pond's Cold Cream was promoted as a way to prevent women working outdoors from developing ruddy complexions and chapped lips. There was also something called 'day lotion' produced by Cyclax, one of the oldest cosmetic companies in Britain. The lotion came in wartime shade choices with bewildering names such as Peach, Light Rachel, Rachel, Deep Rachel, Dark Rachel, Sunburn No 1 and Sunburn No 2. Cyclax also produced a burns cream and a camouflage cream and the company suffered badly in the Blitz when its factory on the Tottenham Court Road was destroyed by enemy action. Surely Hermann Goering was not targeting the cosmetics industry in a bid to ruin British morale?

Chapter Three

A Matter of Conscience

'I say that those people should be made to do jobs, and darned disagreeable jobs, too. Come down to Plymouth and see the sailors and airmen.'

Lady Astor

In January 1940, in a long letter to the *Sunderland Echo*, one V. Miller of Grangetown wrote:

'... the way of the conscientious objector is hard. When life is destructive in its manifestation it is very hard to find a convincing argument that it should be spared ... to be consistent it follows that a "C.O." must not seek to exterminate even the most noxious kind of vermin ... he must be sorely tempted to rebel against his conscience and begin swatting the storm of flies which, in the summer, threaten to poison his foodstuffs ... His nation's body is threatened by a political disease called Nazism, but, unlike his own body's defence forces, he refuses to fight ...'

Just as in the First World War, the issue of the conscientious objector inflamed passions like little else during wartime. This time, just as before, it had been an issue since the very day that war was declared, but in 1940 a man's refusal to join the armed forces for whatever reason – moral, religious or political – brought out the worst in many people. Newspapers reported on tribunals almost daily, the cases so varied in their personnel and circumstances. An Oxford University third-year student, Brian Soper, told his tribunal in Bristol that he had left the Communist Party while still at school and was now an anarchist. He thought all governments were evil and that he would object to paying income tax, and, if he were a motorist, to obeying traffic lights. When the chairman asked him if he really thought that 40 million people could do without a government, he replied, 'Yes.' The chairman, Judge Wethered, said that Soper should try spending a day in a law court. 'Try one of my judgements summons courts. A large number of people really exist on the principle that they will not pay a bill unless they are compelled to do so.' Soper was registered for military service unconditionally.

Twenty-one-year-old Alan Barlow told a Manchester tribunal that it was while he was observing the two-minutes' silence to remember the war dead that he resolved never to assist in the maiming or killing of his fellow beings. That was six years ago, he said. Four years ago he decided that he could not be responsible for killing an animal and so he gave up eating meat. His name was removed from the register.

The mother of one applicant from Rhyl told the tribunal that she would rather shoot her son than see him join the army. Twenty-year-old George Baker was supported by his mother who said that her attitude was the result of a promise made to her husband just before he died in 1919, aged only 26. During the First World War he had served three years in the Army. Mrs Baker said, 'His death was due to his service for his country. I gave him my solemn promise that I would, if possible, prevent our son from joining the Army.' She said that she had fought for almost three years before she was given a pension. Baker said that his father wished for him to have nothing at all to do with war and he had promised never to do so. 'I would rather go to prison than break that promise.' Baker was registered as a conscientious objector on condition that he did agricultural work.

F.G. Barnett, a railway porter from West Ealing, said that he had no obligations to the country and that all he possessed he had worked for. The tribunal's chairman, Mr H.A.L. Fisher, dismissed his appeal against non-combatant service, declaring, 'My experience of young men is that they change their opinions a good deal between 20 and 23.' As he left the room, Barnett turned and said, 'You will never make a soldier out of me.'

When Arthur Healing, a carpenter from Wiltshire, appeared before a Bristol tribunal his father said that even at school his son had the horrors of war driven into his head. 'I've tried many times to get him to change his views on war, but I've always failed.' The case had originally been adjourned so that supporting evidence could be obtained. Healing had said that he did not believe in 'mass murder and the senseless and insane waste of human lives'. 'My idea of life is to save lives, not to take them, to help build a better world not to destroy it.' He said that he would not build a road for guns to go along, and that six or seven months earlier he had given up the chance of one job after finding out that it was on a military camp. He said that for two years he had been a member of the St John Ambulance in Birmingham and was willing to enter the Royal Army Medical Corps but not the Labour Corps, although he had no objection to building canteens for the Army. He was transferred to the military register for non-combatant.

Twenty-year-old G.E.C. Price had been refused admission to both the Royal Navy and the RAF because of his colour. The Edinburgh-born son of a British West Indian, Price was appearing before a tribunal after he refused to register for military service. He told it, 'I was so hurt after my unsuccessful application to join the Navy that I made up my mind never to join up or serve with the British Forces.' His objection now, he said, was that because of the way he had been badly treated, he no longer wanted to fight. Because of his colour he had also found great difficulty in obtaining work. His application for exemption was unconditionally refused, although the chairman of the tribunal, Sheriff C.H. Brown, said, 'I think it right to say that great sympathy was felt by all the members of tribunal, and the decision was not unanimous'.

Conscientious objection split families. The *Britannia and Eve* magazine reported on the case of a widow, since remarried, whose life had been riven apart because her son was a conscientious objector. His father had been killed in the First World War:

'I hardly ever see Harry now. Whether right or wrong, his convictions have made such rifts at home that my husband has forbidden him from the house. Sometimes, when people ask me what Harry is doing, I feel that I would rather say he is dead, out there, where his father died ...'

In February, Judge Ernest Wethered told a Bristol tribunal that he had heard of a British officer who had been warmly thanked by a captured German submarine office for the respectful way in which he had been treated and he would like the Royal Naval officer's name and address, 'so that when we occupy your country I can make sure that you are looked after properly'. The judge related the tale, he said, in order to illustrate what he described as the need to take up a position of reality. 'So many of the applicants that have come before me recently look to be about two years out of date. We have got to stop thinking about this question of war in the abstract.' No doubt that left some panel members scratching their heads.

Francis Dunbar-Marshall, a naturalised British subject of Italian and American parentage, said that he had given up a job as a well-paid military draughtsman in order to act as a handyman – earning 2s 6d pocket money – at a hospital for evacuee children. He was granted exemption on condition that he engaged in ambulance or other humanitarian work.

When it came to those conscientious objectors who had described themselves as agricultural workers and given farm addresses, the *Penrith Observer* wondered how long their association with farming had lasted and why the same address seemed to be so often associated with appeals. Farmers as a class, said the newspaper, were not particularly sympathetic to conscientious objectors because:

> '… the type of mind which leads to this attitude is not usually produced by country conditions or life close to nature. It is very much the product of artificial surroundings and is liable to be found in those who have read more than they can digest … it is irritating to be told that crankiness is a qualification for farm work.'

A writer to another newspaper had likened conscientious objectors to 'people who object to vaccination, and other cranks'.

Passions could run dangerously high. In April 1940, Judge Edward Cooper Burgis almost lost his life after being stabbed in the neck by a man whose application he had dismissed. The day after he had been turned down, Henry Ballantine Best, a 24-year-old clerk, came back to the tribunal as a spectator and interrupted proceedings by clapping loudly. He was ejected, although later readmitted. Later that day, when Judge Burgis was boarding a train at Manchester's London Road station (now Piccadilly station), Best came up behind him and stabbed him several times in the neck and back. Burgis was fortunate to survive. A doctor at Ancoats hospital testified at Best's trial that had the wounds been an inch further to the left or right then they would have proved fatal. Best was found guilty of wounding with intent to murder and was sentenced to five years' penal servitude. In June, Judge Burgis returned to the bench, joking that he felt 'like a casualty on the home front reporting for duty'.

Many employers took a dim view of having a conscientious objector on their payroll. Twenty-two-year James Connor of Southport told a tribunal:

'My employers, with whom I have been since I left school, say that because I am a conscientious objector my services are no longer required. Is this British freedom and justice? Is a man no longer entitled to his opinion? Is he to be branded as a coward because he thinks only in terms of peace?'

Judge Burgis told him, 'You would probably not have the courage to run away. You would go with the others.' But the judge said that Connor as 'very honest', was without qualification and that his name would be removed from the register.

It was not just private concerns that were laying-off those who would not fight. Local authorities followed suit. In January, Cambridgeshire County Council decided that any officer or servant of the council who was registered as a conscientious objector should be given notice to terminate his employment. In May, the Isle of Ely education committee announced that it would dispense with the services of elementary school teachers who had registered as conscientious objectors. In July, Cheshire County Council voted by an overwhelming majority to terminate the contracts of conscientious objectors. Alderman Hodgkinson said that if everyone were a conscientious objector, then 'there would be no liberty'. There were cries of 'Hear, hear,' when he added, 'I don't think that we should employ any conscientious objector.' When it was suggested that wording of the motion might be changed, the town clerk, Mr Scrimgeour, said, 'You could give them leave of absence, but that would mean that they would come back. We don't want to serve with them.' A proposal that the services of conscientious objectors be retained but at soldiers' pay did not received a seconder. The same month, Southport Town Council announced that it was dismissing all employees who had registered, or who would register in the future, as conscientious objectors. Five employees were given their notices immediately, including the town clerk, Mr K.B. Moore, who lost his £550-a-year post.

The decisions by local authorities to sack conscientious objectors were not always unanimous. In May, when Torquay Town Council voted by thirteen votes to seven that no conscientious objector should be employed by any council department, the deputy mayor, Mr A. Denys Phillips, said that the motion cut right across the law of the land and that he could not vote for it. That month, the Co-operative Guild Congress at Great Yarmouth 'viewed with some alarm a tendency of the part of some sections of the working class not to work with conscientious objectors'. The government was asked to instruct military tribunals to ensure equal respect and treatment of political and religious objectors. The congress also asked that any chairman or tribunal member displaying bias against the opinions of an objector should be immediately removed from office.

On 23 February 1940, Lady Astor, the MP for Plymouth Sutton, told the Commons:

'Be kind to the conscientious objector, but not the political objector. The people who do not care for their own country are, like the people who do not care for their own families, no good. If there ever was a war where everybody ought to be made to do his best, it is this war, and I hope the tribunals will be picked with great care, and that we shall get the best of people on them. Be tender with the really spiritually minded, but not with those like the honourable gentleman who said he was not spiritually minded. It is nothing to boast about. In this war we are not only fighting for ourselves, but for civilisation and the things that matter, and you cannot afford to let young men say of others: "They are choosing their own time and have no Christian principles." I say that those people should be made to do jobs, and darned disagreeable jobs, too. Come down to Plymouth and see the sailors and airmen. Last week a sailor told me he had been seventy-six days on a destroyer and had had only three days off. Has the country so little imagination? If they really realised what our people were already doing the government would not need to be so careful not to do this or that. If you would only let the country know what the Navy and Air Force are doing already people would be willing to give up more than they do. I feel for the Christian, but I have no sympathy with those who want to shirk this war and to choose their own fighting.'

In September, the Welsh National Party asked the Ministry of Labour to ensure that where Welsh conscientious objectors were living in England, their cases would be transferred to a Welsh-speaking tribunal. The *Liverpool Echo* commented:

'Already a Welshman in England, who finds difficulty in speaking English, can have his case transferred to a Welsh tribunal. The number affected must be very small and to seek similar facilities for all who desire them is to exaggerate the importance of what is a minor matter. It is just that a man who has difficulty with English should have his case heard where he can make himself clearly understood, and his interest is already adequately safeguarded.'

In July, Professor W.J. Gruffydd, writing in the quarterly Welsh-language literary journal *Y LLenor*, exhorted Welshmen to join up:

'Britain is fighting for her life. Everything that has been cherished in Wales will be lost if Hitler adds to the destruction he has already caused. Nobody brought up in the Liberal and humanitarian traditions of Wales could live in a country conquered by him or by the craven Mussolini, or the pseudo-religious Franco.'

The *Liverpool Echo* said that it would not be surprised to see a number of Welsh conscientious objectors change their attitude on reading Professor Gruffydd's words.

In January a member of the Bruderhof Christian community in the Cotswolds told a tribunal that he objected to war service because 'to my mind you cannot use evil to destroy evil'. The Bruderhof, which consisted of Germans, French, Swiss, Poles and other nationalities, had fled Germany some years before and were living at Ashton Keynes in Wiltshire. Its members led a simple life and grew and sold food locally. Faced with local hostility, the Bruderhof said that they did not trade for profit. Residents presented a petition to the Home Secretary, protesting at the freedom allowed to German members of the Bruderhof, and then dairymen complained that the Bruderhof had recently bought two milk-retailing businesses in Swindon, whereupon the local Conservative MP, William Wavell Wakefield, a former England Rugby Union captain – for forty-three years he was the country's most capped player – severely criticised the Bruderhof, who he claimed were stealing the business interests of local men who had been conscripted. Wakefield, who had served at a Royal Naval Air Service testing station on Windermere during the First World War, said:

'I have no sympathy with you. While others are fighting and suffering hardship, members of your brotherhood are conscientious objectors, and are trying to pinch the business interests of men called to the Colours. We are engaged in a life or death struggle, but you do nothing except hide behind our fighting men. As for taking another man's business while he or his assistants are in the Forces, that is a thing I shall fight with all my power.'

None of the Bruderhof had so far been interned. 'We are carrying on as usual,' said one of them. Later in 1940, however, the government confronted them with options: to accept the internment of its German nationals; or leave the country. Determined to remain together, almost all members of the community – mostly city-raised Europeans – emigrated to Paraguay. Three members remained in England to rebuild the community as dozens of newcomers continued to arrive.

As 1940 went on and the war came closer to home, some men changed their minds about joining up. In June, just after the Dunkirk evacuation had been completed, Reginald Brake, a 20-year-old student teacher from Chester, asked if his status as a conscientious objector could be revoked. Recent events, he said, had made him change his mind. He now felt that he could not stand aside in this crisis and, having qualified as a wireless operator, he wished to join the RAF. The chairman said that young Brake had made a courageous decision and that the tribunal would take what steps it could to see that he could fulfil his desire.

Arthur Livett, a tailor's machinist who was employed at the Royal Arsenal, asked for his name to be crossed off as a conscientious objector. 'My wife was expecting a baby, and that and worry about money was playing on my mind.' His name was removed from the register.

In June one young man told a meeting sponsored by the lord mayor of Sheffield that he had ceased to be a conscientious objector as a result of meeting Moral Re-Armament (MRA), the nondenominational revivalistic movement that by 1938 had evolved from American churchman Frank N.D. Buchman's Oxford Group which held the root of all problems to be fear and selfishness:

> 'When I originally registered it was as a conscientious objector. But when I listened to God, after meeting MRA, I saw that my real motive was the fear of the danger and hardship of service life. I am now ready to serve my country in any capacity and have removed my name from the register.'

Ironically, in 1940 when the new Minister of Labour, Ernest Bevin, decided to conscript the twenty-nine MRA workers in Britain who had previously been exempted from military service, over 2,500 clergy and ministers signed a petition opposing this and 174 Members of Parliament supported them by putting their names to a motion. Bevin made clear that he would resign if he was defeated, and the government put a three-line whip on the supporters of the MRA's position. As it happened, that was unnecessary because George Mathers, the Labour MP for Linlithgowshire and the rebel MPs' spokesman, had already announced that they would not call for a vote but would instead rely on Bevin to recognise the justice of their case. The twenty-nine were still excluded from the Exemption from Military Service Bill.

In April, when during a debate at the National Conservative and Unionist Association conference at the Central Hall, Westminster, a uniformed Army officer defended the rights of conscientious objectors, Tory women rose to hiss at him. Second-Lieutenant Ernest Harrison, who before the war had been the Conservative candidate for Houghton-le-Spring, was speaking against a resolution condemning the activities of peace organisations. 'I do not agree with the conscientious objector,' he said:

> 'but in the name of all that is sacred and English they have a right to their conscience. I am very unhappy about the spirit that is developing in this country. Two years ago, if I said that it was better for ninety-nine shirkers to escape conscription than for one real objector to be forced to fight, everyone in the Conservative Party would have clapped and said: "Hear, hear." After seven months of war we have developed this wicked, intolerant attitude ... I maintain that if you are living in England you have a perfect right to disapprove of the war.'

Another delegate, Private B.R. Brain, who was wearing battledress, disagreed with his superior officer. 'I accuse the Peace Pledge Union of being the tool, unwittingly, of Berlin. It should be supressed.' On 28 May 1940, just seven weeks after he had been condemned for speaking out in support of conscientious objectors, 29-year-old Second-Lieutenant Ernest Harrison of 11th Battalion, Durham Light Infantry, was killed in action in France.

On 20 November 1940, the Ministry of Labour announced that the number provisionally registered as conscientious objectors was: England 1,505; Scotland 228; Wales 141. That represented 0.51 per cent of the total eligible for service in the armed force.

Chapter Four

Careless Talk ...

'The casual gossip, especially between strangers on blacked-out trains, is often criminally dangerous.'

The Bystander magazine

In February 1940, a press conference chaired by Sir Kenneth Lee, the director general of the Ministry of Information, released details of the government's new anti-gossip campaign. Thanks to the distribution of 2.25 million posters, the phrase 'Careless talk costs lives' would soon be familiar to everyone. The posters were stuck on billboards in streets and on railway stations and they hung in pubs and cafes. They appeared in practically every national newspaper, in most regional papers and there were even in two in the United States. A Cabinet paper by Sir John Reith, the Minister of Information, kept secret at the time, covered the initiatives behind the campaign that was fronted by the series of posters that were illustrated by 'Fougasse', the pen name of Cyril Bird, art editor of *Punch* magazine, who produced the artwork for free.

There was more to the campaign than posters, however. Warning lectures would be given to men in all three of the armed services and the Brewers' Society was co-operating by writing to all public house licensees asking them to warn their customers against indiscreet gossip. Certain 'responsible people' were being encouraged to write to newspapers giving instances of the dangers of gossip. Ten 'anti-gossip' talks were broadcast by the BBC, public speakers were asked to mention the anti-gossip campaign wherever possible and well-known writers including Agatha Christie, Somerset Maugham and E.M. Delafield were asked to supply articles on the results of careless talk.

The film industry was also involved. From mid-March, three short flickering black and white films made by the Ministry of Information and distributed by Metro-Goldwyn-Meyer were released fortnightly to 2,000 cinemas. The intention was to show how the smallest scrap of careless talk could lead to the most monumental disaster. In *All Hands*, a sailor, played by John Mills, casually tells his sweetheart the date on which his warship would sail. The manageress of the café that they are in overhears this. She is spying for the Germans and the ship is later torpedoed and sunk. Another film, *Dangerous Comment*, portrayed how a bombing raid had to be cancelled because a depressed pilot had mentioned it to his equally depressed fiancée. A barman, a spy, passes the message on to a contact, who tips off the Luftwaffe, but fortunately a security officer was also present and the raid is called off and the spy arrested. The third film, *Now You're Talking*, shows Alf, a disgruntled worker, inadvertently informing another enemy agent in a pub that he has had to work late because there is some overnight research being carried out on a captured enemy aircraft. Saboteurs blow up the factory. The film ends with Alf propping up the same bar and wondering how it all happened. 'You know what? Somebody taking too much …' *The Times* questioned the psychology of the films; they were effectively thrillers – and fast-paced well-produced thrillers at that – but did people believe in them or did thrillers, because they were fiction, automatically induce disbelief?

The message certainly resonated with newspapers. A writer in the *Birmingham Post* related how on a train journey a business friend had fallen into conversation with a 'charming elderly man' who said that he was a director of a large industrial concern. The friend told his new acquaintance that he was curious to see how local blast furnaces complied with blackout regulations. His companion suggested switching off the carriage lights and opening the blind and then proceeded to identify landmarks and talk freely about the new war industries and defence establishments that had appeared recently. As they parted, the friend told the man, 'It's a good job I'm not a German spy!' The old man blanched and replied, 'God bless my soul, you aren't are you?'

The *Daily Record* said that the danger was 'real and vital':

'How real is obvious from the fact that Britain is to launch its anti-gossip campaign today. The urgency of the problem is brought home more forcibly by the fact that every day men on leave from the BEF are coming home and often asked ridiculous questions which if only for the sake of politeness they must answer in some way. Without thinking they may easily give away vital information that someone standing by, who is only waiting for a chance to help the enemy, may overhear and pass on ...'

The Birmingham-based *Evening Despatch* warned its readers, 'Who Knows? Hitler May Be Under The Breakfast Table.' It described the posters:

'... an omnipotent, all-hearing Hitler, crouching under bus seats and on luggage racks, or lurking in barracks. His ears are glued to every telephone kiosk; the pattern of every wallpaper weaves itself into a mosaic of dropping locks and toothbrush moustaches to show that even walls have ears ...'

A letter writer to the same newspaper picked up the theme. R.H Fairbairn said:

'Everyone is acquainted with the poster 'Careless Talk May Give Away Secrets', yet on the bus the other day passengers heard a soldier remark to an Air Force man: "Where are you at?" "On the East Coast, Where are you?" "On the Firth of Forth." It's the same in public houses: vital information being given away.'

The *Birmingham Daily Gazette* said that on 'provincial journeys a colleague had heard more details of shipping and troop movements (even from members of the Military Police!) than he has ever heard in Fleet Street.' The writer continued, 'Travelling from the Midlands I have myself been treated to facts about the manufacture and operation of secret aircraft by a complete stranger. In buses I have heard conversations about troop trains.'

The *Liverpool Echo* thought that the worst nuisance was the person who pretended to know more than was ever made public:

'He is better informed than the Cabinet and he has got it straight from the horse's mouth This type is to be met in pubs and clubs and wherever men congregate. Vanity leads him into indiscretions and though he is both a fool and a bore, he can do harm among credulous people who are ready and willing to believe anything. Maybe he is of little or no use to the enemy, but he may have a demoralising influence on the home front, and he must be made to keep his mouth shut.'

The *Western Morning News* hoped that men in service centres such as Plymouth and in establishments like the Royal Dockyards would pay particular attention to the campaign. 'A few words of gossip such as "Her brother is going to Gibraltar next Sunday," might mean the loss of 2,000 lives in the sinking of a troopship'. Plymouth's lady mayoress and a local MP, Lady Astor, made an impassioned plea. 'Do not think for a moment that spies are German. Of course they are not; they are English. You do not use foreigners to do your spying, and one cannot be too careful.' Referring to the arrival of HMS *Exeter* that in December 1939 had engaged the German pocket battleship the *Admiral Graf Spee* in the Battle of the River Plate, off Montevideo, she said that she had heard from people some distance from Plymouth two days before the *Exeter* arrived that the cruiser was coming. 'Suppose that from carelessness the Germans had got to know the exact time that the *Exeter* was coming ... Even if you do hear anything, keep it to yourself. Do not pass it on to the next person.'

The Bystander magazine felt that the Careless Talk initiative had not come a moment too soon:

'The casual gossip, especially between strangers on blacked-out trains, is often criminally dangerous. And, of course, the patriotic Englishman, overhearing such gossip, is instinctively averse to making a scene and telling the gossipers to shut up. But he ought to, all the same.'

There was always someone prepared to make a commercial advantage out of such things. By the end of February, newspapers were carrying an advertisement that advised people, 'Don't Spread Rumours, Spread Velveeta – the delicious cheese food that spreads like butter.'

Chapter Five

This is the BBC Forces Programme ...

'It's being so cheerful as keeps me going'

Mona Lott, *ITMA*

As life on the Home Front became much more difficult and dangerous, entertainment became increasingly important in providing some form of escape, however fleeting. Information, too, was vital. The BBC's radio broadcasts provided both. Upon the outbreak of war, the BBC had merged its National Programme and various regional programmes into one, calling it the BBC Home Service, providing news, public information and music. As the months went by and troops found themselves in barracks, both in France and at home, with nothing much to do, in February 1940 the BBC launched its Forces Programme to provide popular music, comedy, drama and general variety shows. The civilian population could also hear this rich mixture of entertainment and it was proving more popular than the Home Service. So after France fell and the war came much closer to Britain, the BBC decided to continue broadcasting the Forces programme to the entire United Kingdom. It was now the light entertainment station of choice for the nation.

Initially, the Forces Programme aired from 11am to 11pm daily, but from 16 June 1940 it began at 6.30am every day. Programmes that had been designed for specific services, such as *Garrison Theatre*, which starred Jack Warner, for the army, and *Ack Ack Beer Beer*, which featured Wing Commander Kenneth Horne, for anti-aircraft units, barrage balloon stations and coastal artillery, soon became essential listening for civilians too. Harry S. Pepper and Charles Shadwell, who had been an entertainments officer in the West Yorkshire Regiment during the First World War, devised *Garrison Theatre*. Pepper and Shadwell created a radio version of the homespun revues that had entertained troops on the Western Front between 1914 and 1918. Invited audiences of service men and women soon recreated the raucous atmosphere of those earlier times. Jack Warner's regular 'Letter from Syd', in which he read out letters purporting to be from his brother who was serving in France, proved immensely popular. Sometimes an obvious expletive was replaced with the words 'blue pencil', which delighted Warner's audience who were all too familiar with the censor.

The pre-war *Band Waggon* – the first comedy show to be designed specifically for radio – starring Arthur Askey and Richard 'Stinker' Murdoch continued in popularity until the middle of 1940 when it ended because Murdoch joined the RAF, while Askey went off to pursue a film career.

On Sunday, 24 May 1940, as the evacuation from Dunkirk got under way, a new radio show aired on the Forces Programme. *Hi Gang!* was the idea of American film actor Ben Lyon who, with his actress wife, Bebe Daniels, had been travelling around Britain entertaining troops and workers alike in theatres, army camps and factories. Lyon suggested to the BBC's head of light entertainment, Pat Hillyard, that a light comedy programme on radio would reach so many more people all at the same time and would help to boost morale as the war took a disturbing new turn. Austrian-born British actor and comedian Vic Oliver agreed to join them. Daniels wrote most of the script, there was a new song every week and the show delighted its audience by poking fun at Hitler and at Lord Haw Haw, the Irish-German anti-British propagandist whose voice was now as familiar on the wireless as that of any comedian. *Hi Gang!* would see out the war and continue being broadcast until 1949.

In June 1940 the *Radio Times* announced:

'This coming week there will be, twice every day, half an hour's music meant specially for factory workers to listen to as they work. You will find it in the programme pages for each day under the title Music While You Work.'

And so, at 10.30am on Sunday, 23 June 1940, a new half-hour radio programme began on the BBC. It first aired on the Home Service that day, and featured the theatre organist Dudley Beaven. The second edition went out at 3pm that afternoon, on the Forces Programme when it was sandwiched between *All Sorts of Music,* in which gramophone records were played, and a variety show starring, among others, Cyril Fletcher and Morton Fraser 'from the stage of a cinema'.

On that first day, newspaper listings applied the name *Music While You Work* to only the afternoon slot, which featured a trio, the Organolians, with Harry Farmer playing the Hammond organ, Jack Moss the drums, and Jimmy Leach the piano. Leach would later take over the organ and the band, and in September 1967 Jimmy Leach and his Organolians would play the final tune of the final edition of *Music While You Work*.

Back in June 1940, however, at the same time as the Organolians were getting into the swing of things, the Home Service offered a concert featuring the BBC Orchestra (Section B) followed by a talk from the Very Reverend F.A. Iremonger entitled 'From a Deanery Window'. As *Music While You Work* was the result of a suggestion by the government, that if cheerful music was piped into the nation's factories then it would improve morale and thus lead to better production, it is unlikely that, on this Sunday afternoon, many munitions factories were opting for the bass tones of Norman Walker and a talk about religious books and events.

Music While You Work was to be broadcast in two half-hour programmes daily, one at 10.30am and the other in the middle of the afternoon, halfway through shifts when production might be flagging. A different band, orchestra or ensemble would play each day and the best choice of music would be that which encouraged workers to whistle or sing along. A great deal of thought went into each playlist. At the best of times factories can be noisy environments, and the music played over a public-address system had to be loud as well as of a constant pitch. The tempo also had to be just right. Nothing too slow, obviously, but nothing too fast either. It was felt that this might unsettle workers. So the BBC issued a set of rules to which producers had to strictly adhere.

Banned completely were: numbers with predominant rhythm, insufficient melody, or other unsuitable characteristics; numbers that were lethargic or unsuited to any speeding up of tempo; all modern slow waltzes, due to their soporific tendencies. There was also a list of numbers that were deemed unsuitable for other reasons, such as *Deep in the Heart of Texas* whose clapping motif, it was felt, would encourage workers to bang their spanners on the machinery, causing damage to the same. Initially, *Music While You Work* had different signature and signing-off tunes but in October 1940 it adopted permanently for both *Calling All Workers*, composed by Eric Coates whose name would one day become synonymous with the *Dam Busters March*. Eventually, as 24-hour shifts were introduced in armaments factories, *Music While You Work* was broadcast three times daily.

The programme was a huge success and by the end of the war more than 9,000 factories broadcast it through loudspeakers to workers. The *BBC Year Book* for 1941 commented:

'Programmes of music for factory workers have been broadcast since the end of June as a help to lessen strain, relieve monotony, and thereby increase efficiency. The initiative came from the factories, and in collaboration with recognised authorities the BBC carried out research among workers to discover their preferences, and among factories to establish their special needs. The result was the mid-morning and mid-afternoon programmes *Music While You Work*.'

The radio show that, it seemed, everyone did not want to miss was *It's That Man Again*, or *ITMA* as it was universally known. The show had begun broadcasting on 12 July 1939, initially as four shows to be aired fortnightly. It took its name from the ever-increasing use of that phrase during the early month of 1939 to describe Hitler, specifically in a *Daily Express* headline of 2 May 1939, written by Bert Gunn who had begun to use it when talking about the increasingly alarming behaviour of the Fuhrer on the international stage. New Zealand-born Ted Kavanagh wrote the *ITMA* scripts which generally followed the adventures of Tommy Handley, a variety artist and himself a scriptwriter who during the First World War had served in a kite balloon section of the Royal Naval Air Service.

Handley was already a veteran of radio entertainment, having worked in the medium in its infancy. Now he was to become a national treasure as he undertook a number of bizarre posts, fictional of course, such as Minister of Aggravation and Mysteries at the Office of Twerps; the mayor of a down-at-heel seaside resort called Foaming-at-the-Mouth;

and Governor of a South Sea island, Tomtopia. There were characters such as Colonel Humphrey Chinstrap, a permanently sozzled former Indian Army officer who, no matter what the question, assumed that he was being offered a drink and always replied, 'I don't mind if I do!' Jack Train, who based it on someone he had known, played the character.

'I don't mind if I do!' became a catchphrase repeated in homes, shops, factories and pubs across the nation. Others caught on too: 'Can I do you now, sir?' spoken by Dorothy Summers' character, a cleaner called Mrs Mopp; 'Don't forget the diver,' spoken by Horace Percival who entered and exited as a diver; 'It's being so cheerful as keeps me going,' the words of Mona Lott, a depressed laundrywoman played by Joan Harben; 'This is Funf speaking,' a German spy also played by Jack Train. And, perhaps the most used of all – 'TTFN' ('Ta ta for now'). *ITMA* would run for more than 300 episodes to January 1949, when the irreplaceable Handley died after suffering a brain haemorrhage.

When it came to providing the nation with information, thanks to an agreement with the newspaper industry the BBC had never broadcast news before 7pm. But with war clouds gathering, on 25 August 1939 daily morning and lunchtime news bulletins were added and for the first time listeners became acquainted with the names of newsreaders who they now needed to trust as never before. Alvar Liddell, born in Surrey of Swedish parents, had introduced Neville Chamberlain when he told the nation that it was now at war with Germany. 'Here is the news, and this is Alvar Liddell reading it,' became another catchphrase. John Snagge, a voice already well known as the commentator for the Oxford-Cambridge Boat Race, became the BBC's presentation director, making announcements of national importance as the war unfolded. Former singer Frank Phillips was another voice to become familiar to millions as his unmistakable baritone announced the ever-changing tide of war. On 26 January 1936, Stuart Hibberd had delivered the words, 'The King's life is moving peacefully towards it close.' He, too, now became a vital link.

The BBC was not just speaking to the Home Front. In between the normal programmes of music, comedy and drama, radio listings now carried items such as 'The News in German' and 'The News in Norwegian'. Behind that was a major development for the BBC, whose pre-war Empire Service had, since November 1939, been known as the Overseas Service. Staffing for non-domestic output had risen from 103 in 1939 to almost 1,500 by the end of 1940. In December 1940, a landmine exploded outside Broadcasting House, causing a fire that blazed for seven hours. As a result, the Overseas Service was moved a few miles away, to a disused skating rink in Maida Vale. But it had a glass roof and so some sections were moved again, this time to Wood Norton Hall in Worcestershire, which the BBC bought in 1939 as a relocation centre. The European services, though, were transferred back to London, to Bush House between Aldwych and the Strand and near to Fleet Street, then the heart of the British newspaper industry. By the end of 1940, the BBC was broadcasting in thirty-four languages. Each day, seventy-eight news bulletins were broadcast, and new services included Icelandic, Albanian, Hindi, Burmese and the dialect of Luxembourg. Danish and Norwegian language news bulletins had begun in April 1940, on the day the two countries were invaded; the service in Dutch began a month after Holland was occupied in May. Because Belgium's population was divided into two language areas – French and Flemish – each language was featured on alternate nights. The German service posed a particular dilemma because it made use of refugees and it was felt that German listeners would assume that they were therefore Jewish. The BBC also did not want to give the impression that it was broadcasting propaganda promoted by refugees but that it was 'the sincere expression of an English point of view'. This was all also available to listeners sitting by their own British firesides, in the unlikely event that they would tune-in in preference to Ben Lyon and Bebe Daniels taking aim at Lord Haw.

Listening to William Joyce himself was another matter. The man who was, according to American journalist William Shirer, 'the war's outstanding radio traitor' had received a contract as a newsreader at the *Reichs-Rundfunk-Gesellschaft* (Reich Broadcasting Corporation) on 18 September 1939, a week after making his first broadcast to Britain, after which the *Daily Express* radio critic, Jonah Barrington (real name Cyril Carr Dalmaine), had written:

'A gent I'd like to meet is moaning periodically from Zeesen [the German radio station beaming overseas broadcasts]. He speaks

English of the haw–haw, damit-get-out-of-my-way variety, and his strong suit is gentlemanly indignation.'

The identity of Lord Haw Haw caused endless speculation – and anger. On 19 October 1939, the *News Review* magazine published a letter from Mr A.R. Thomas of Bournemouth, who described Lord Haw Haw's broadcast as 'nauseating' and 'disgusting', and wondered how, if he were an Englishman, he could behave 'in such a sickening, renegade manner'. *News Review* got it wrong in saying that Lord Haw Haw was a man called Hoffman who just happened to be married to a Manchester girl and now lived in Munich. Barrington, meanwhile, had continued his attack on the broadcaster who he imagined to have 'a monocle, a vacant eye, a gardenia in his buttonhole. Rather like P.G. Wodehouse's Bertie Wooster'. Alas, Barrington's efforts to bring down Lord Haw Haw with a barrage of mockery had the opposite effect. Instead he was in danger of becoming the radio personality of the Second World War. Smith's Electric Clocks ran an advertisement with a drawing of a monocled donkey at the microphone with the caption 'Don't risk missing Haw-Haw. Get a clock that shows the right time always, unquestionably.'

In fact Lord Haw Haw was William Brooke Joyce, a 34-year-old American-born Anglo-Irish Fascist. His father was Irish; his mother came from Lancashire. A former member of Oswald Moseley's British Union of Fascists, Joyce had fled with his wife to Germany in August 1939, after learning that the British intended to detain him under Defence Regulations. He took German citizenship in 1940. Listening to his broadcasts (which were always prefaced by 'Germany calling, Germany calling, Germany calling') was discouraged but not illegal. Early in 1940, on behalf of both the Ministry of Information and Mass Observation, the BBC undertook a study of German broadcasts. According to its findings, at the end of January 1940, one out of every six adults was a regular listener, three were occasional listeners, and two never listened. At the same time, four out of every six people were listening regularly to the BBC News. In February 1940, as a counter-measure, the eminent lawyer Norman Birkett, who would serve as the alternate British judge at the Nuremberg War Trials, went on air to refute many of Lord Haw Haw's claims about damage to British cities, shipping and so on. His efforts did not do much to reduce the listening figures of William Joyce who was, according to a letter writer to *Illustrated* magazine, 'funnier than anything the BBC ever put on'. Joyce, though, enjoyed his popularity mostly while there was inaction on the battlefield and in the skies over Britain. Once the Phoney War was over, whatever tolerance he might have enjoyed from British radio listeners ended with it. He was hanged on 3 January 1946, the last person to be executed for treason in the United Kingdom.

For those who wanted to leave the fireside, there was the cinema and the theatre. Cinemas in particular were packed, people watching films through a blue haze of cigarette smoke. In the early days of 1940, if an air-raid warning sounded then the manager would appear in front of the screen to announce the danger. Most people chose to remain in their seats and wait for the film to restart. Eventually, the warning was flashed on to the screen so that the film was not interrupted. During the Blitz, cinemas became regarded as safe havens. Unless they received a direct hit they offered good shelter, especially under the balcony to where many patrons retreated once the alarm was given. There was a wide choice of British films in 1940. Over eighty were released that year, ranging from *Under Your Hat* starring the husband and wife team, Jack Hulbert and Cicely Courtneidge, to *That's The Ticket* with Sid Field, and *Night Train to Munich* with Rex Harrison and Margaret Lockwood. The government was involving itself in helping the British film industry overcome wartime conditions. On 10 July 1940, under the Defence Regulations, it introduced a voluntary scheme where filmmakers would spend at least £1,000 on British labour and services for every 1,000ft of 'quota' film (the 1938 Film Quota Act required distributors to use at least 22 per cent of British films) and there must be at least one British film of not less than 700ft for every 100,000ft of foreign film. The government hoped that the optional system would encourage British producers to concentrate '100 per cent' on British films.

It was, however, Hollywood films that proved most popular in 1940. In December *The Great Dictator*, in which Charlie Chaplin played both leading roles – a fascist dictator and a persecuted Jewish barber – delighted British filmgoers with is satire. But the smash hit of the year was *Gone With The Wind*, starring the young English actress Vivien Leigh. In January 1940, the *Daily Record* said that the film was 'unlikely, according to rumour, to be shown in this country until after the war. It has cost a fortune to make, of course, and presumably the feeling is that its earnings in Britain in wartime would be less than in peacetime'. However, *Gone With The Wind* opened in London on 18 April that year, at three West End cinemas, the Empire, the Palace and the Ritz. According to the *Daily Herald* film critic P.L. Mannock, the four-hour film was 'worth every second of the time … the most stupendous film yet made … a tremendous emotional experience'. The *Manchester Guardian* was quite unsure, however. On 28 May 1940 it said of *Gone With The Wind*, '… its story lacks the epic quality which alone could justify such a lavish outlay of time, talent, and production values'.

On 4 September 1939 the government had banned the assembly of large crowds and closed down all theatres and cinemas, along with sporting venues, because they feared aerial bombardment. The closures had hardly come as a surprise; in October that year, the editor of *Theatre World* wrote that 'the grave dislocation of the theatre industry throughout the country, with its attendant distress and unemployment, was not unforeseen'. But the bombing had not materialised and soon cinemas and theatres were again open for business. The authorities realised that people needed entertainment to lift their spirits. When the ban was lifted on 12 September, initially just a few West End theatres decided to reopen, along with suburban and provincial theatres, but by the summer of 1940, more and more were playing to packed houses

At the end of 1939, theatre producer Basil Dean had set up the Entertainments National Service Association (ENSA) to provide entertainment for British forces. By 1940, ENSA was organising concerts for civilian workers as well as for troops. Meanwhile, Kenneth Clarke, who was then in charge of the National Gallery, felt that the public needed not just any old entertainment 'of the film or music-hall order' and that the government should 'take some active part in stimulating activities of this sort'. In January 1940, the Council for the Encouragement of Music and the Arts (CEMA) was set up to support the arts during wartime. It would prove to be the forerunner of the post-war Arts Council. Originally a private initiative to promote classical music, drama, opera and ballet, especially to new audiences, CEMA was later sponsored by the government. Funds were raised to help drama groups and music societies continue to operate despite wartime restrictions. The National Gallery had been empty since Clarke had overseen the removal of its artworks upon the outbreak of war, but in 1940 it became the venue for a series of lunchtime concerts, some of them given by the famous pianist Myra Hess, whose idea it had been to provide Londoners with a dose of culture during their lunch breaks. These proved so popular that during air-raids they continued in the basement, on one occasion even after a bomb exploded nearby.

The effort to introduce a bit of high-class culture to ordinary people was laudable but many still wanted the kind of entertainment offered by establishments like the Windmill Theatre which sat in the heart of Soho and offered a series of *tableaux vivants*. Nude showgirls posed, portraying scenes such as Britannia, mermaids and Native Americans (or Red Indians as they were known). They would remain motionless, as the law demanded, although there were some inventive ways around this, such as a nude girl clinging to a spinning rope. Again, the shows proved enormously popular – the audiences were, of course, exclusively male – and the Windmill girls performed throughout the Blitz, giving rise to the theatre's famous motto 'We Never Closed' (other than during those September days of 1939 when all theatres were forced to shut their doors). The motto was sometimes humorously modified to 'We Never Clothed' and the Windmill encapsulated much of the spirit of London in 1940.

Chapter Six

The Game Should Be Kept Going

'No one knew what was going to happen in the war. It wasn't easy to concentrate on football '

Frank Broome, Aston Villa and England

In September 1940, Richmond Golf Club in Surrey conceded that 'In all competitions, during gunfire, or when bombs are falling, players may take cover without penalty for ceasing play.' However, another rule said, 'A player whose stroke is affected by simultaneous explosion of bomb or shell, or by machine-gun fire, may play the ball from the same place. Penalty: 1 stroke.' A typical example of golfers' sang-froid was shown by the following rules, 'The position of known delayed action bombs are marked by red flags at a reasonable – but not guaranteed – safe distance therefrom.' And 'A ball moved by enemy action may be placed as near as possible where it lay, or if lost or destroyed, a ball may be dropped not nearer the hole, without penalty.'

Whether Richmond's rules revisions were serious, or whether they were meant simply to amuse, they were republished in several newspapers in the United States as a classic example of British pluck and resilience. Whichever the case, sport certainly had to adapt in the first year of the war when, in particular, cricket, football and horseracing were badly affected.

The National Hunt season had already been hit by the savage winter that saw meeting after meeting abandoned. The weather, though, did not prevent a large body of British racegoers braving the Irish Sea to be at Leopardstown on 20 January 1940 for the Red Cross Handicap Chase – reportedly 'the most valuable race ever staged in Ireland' – that was held in connection with a sweepstake for the benefit of the Irish Red Cross Society and authorised by a special Act of the Irish Parliament. Conditions at the course were dreadful, but the BBC radio commentator,

Raymond Glendenning, was unable to tell listeners that he could not see large parts of the race. Defence regulations forbade him from reporting on the weather.

Back home it was suggested that, in order to limit the strain on public transport, the Jockey Club might restrict race meetings to Saturdays and Bank Holidays and hold them either in 'country places' where large crowds were unlikely, or else near large population centres. Colonel W.B. Vince of the Air Raid Protection Department had an original idea – attendances could be restricted if race meetings were made less interesting than normal.

In February, the Home Office agreed that the 1940 Grand National could be run at Aintree as usual, despite a letter from Captain A.F. Hordern, the chief constable of Lancashire, who strongly opposed the idea. He pointed out that the attendance would probably number around 25,000 and that there were practically no air-raid shelters for them. If there were an attack, then Aintree's stands and enclosure would make perfect targets for enemy bombers. In the event, the crowd turned up but the Luftwaffe stayed away. The race was won by Bogskar, a 25/1 shot ridden by RAF sergeant Mervyn Jones.

The annual Cheltenham Festival was reduced to two days' racing, but Easter 1940 saw the biggest racing weekend of the entire war. In May, with the BEF in full retreat to the Channel ports, the chief constable of East Sussex asked whether the forthcoming meeting at Lewes, which was less than 9 miles from Newhaven – the main base for British hospital ships operating between England and France – could be cancelled because he did not wish to spare police officers for a race meeting. The Dunkirk evacuation was in full swing when he was told that 'it is the policy of Government that racing should, for the present, continue to the extent to which it has hitherto been permitted'. And so, as British soldiers were being evacuated from France, racing went ahead at Lewes, and also at Bath, Salisbury and Hurst Park.

With Epsom racecourse commandeered by the military towards the end of 1939, meetings there were abandoned until further notice. So, where to stage the 1940 Epsom Classics? Newbury was considered but there was strong opposition from the local council. The meeting was transferred to the summer course at Newmarket. Over 12 and 13 June, the 'New Derby Stakes' and the 'New Oaks Stakes' were run there. A crowd of more than 10,000, hundreds of them walking from the town centre, saw the Derby. Many came in special coaches, clogging local roads, while two special trains brought 1,400 punters from King's Cross. It was too late for the government to have second thoughts about allowing the meeting, but a late decision was made to discourage publicity for it. Thus, the BBC cancelled its radio commentary, substituting it with a documentary entitled *A Visit to an Arms Factory*.

As war came ever closer, racecourses were requisitioned to provide temporary accommodation for the troops returning from France. Ascot, Cheltenham, Aintree and Haydock Park were all pressed into service, while jockeys were also doing their bit. In September 1940, what was thought to be a German airman shot down over Northamptonshire found himself marched to the nearest police station by a Home Guard who also happened to be a National Hunt jockey and trainer by the name of Cliff Beechener. In fact the 'airman' was a spy who had been knocked out as he was parachuting into deepest Northants. Swedish-born Gösta Caroli was turned into a double-agent by MI5, although he was later judged to be too much trouble to be of any use. Forty years later, Beechener said that his captive had been wearing orange leather shoes 'and it occurred to me that I would not think much of a chap who wore shoes like that'. On Boxing Day 1940, meetings were held at Taunton and Wetherby, followed by Nottingham on 30 December. As John Saville says in his book *Insane and Unseemly*, 'Racing at the end of 1940 was like Dr Johnson's dog walking on its hind legs: it is not done well but you are surprised to find it done at all.'

Reviewing the 1939 cricket season in *Wisden Cricketers' Almanack*, author R. C. Robertson-Glasgow, the Oxford Blue who had played for Somerset from 1920 to 1935, wrote that it was 'like peeping curiously through the wrong end of a telescope at a very small but very happy world'. Also writing in that 1940 edition of *Wisden*, Harry Altham, the former Oxford University, Surrey and Hampshire cricketer who was awarded the MC and DSO while serving as a major in the 60th Rifles during the First World War, described his 'sobering experience' after visiting Lord's in December 1939:

'... there were sandbags everywhere, and the Long Room was stripped and bare with its treasures safely stored beneath the ground, but ... one felt that somehow it would take more than a totalitarian war to stop cricket ... the game can and should be kept going whenever possible.'

As far back as 15 June 1938, a David Low cartoon in the London *Evening Standard* had depicted Prime Minister Neville Chamberlain as a quivering batsman defending a wicket that was the Rock of Gibraltar. In conference at the other end were Hitler, Mussolini and Franco. They were about to bowl Chamberlain a hand grenade. Fourteen months later, on Wednesday, 30 August 1939, six County Cricket Championship matches got under way. Two days later, Germany invaded Poland and the cricket season stuttered to a halt.

But then nothing much happened and in the spring of 1940 there was talk of a limited County Championship being staged that summer. At that point, only men between the ages of 20 and 23 were called up for military service. That left the majority of pre-war professional cricketers available for their counties.

A few days before the season was to start, Germany attacked Norway and Denmark. A month later it was the turn of France, Holland and Belgium. Even then, some in the game were undaunted. Hedley Verity, the Yorkshire left-arm spinner who was training with the Green Howards in Richmond, North Yorkshire, told readers of *The Cricketer* magazine that the Nazi invasion of Holland was 'an early-season setback'. On 21 July 1943, 38-year-old Captain Verity would be killed after being hit in the chest by shrapnel while leading his troops against the Germans in Sicily.

The Oval had been commandeered in 1939 and made ready as a prisoner-of-war camp, although no prisoners were ever held there. At Lord's, the adjoining Nursery End was used by the RAF's 903 Squadron Balloon Barrage. Many buildings at the Pavilion End were put to use as the RAF's No.1 Aircrew Reception Area that received raw recruits. On 16 October 1940, at the height of the Blitz, an oil bomb fell near the sightscreen at the Nursery End. When the bomb burst open it revealed a photograph of a young German officer, bearing the message 'With compliments.' The same year, a barrage balloon cable became snagged on the ground's famous Father Time weather vane that fell into seats in the Grandstand. Lord's was also used as an Auxiliary Fire Station. Meanwhile, in the committee room at Lord's, the MCC was holding its 1940 annual general meeting. It was agreed that this exclusive club could now accept new members over and above the peacetime 300 per year, to compensate for the unusual conditions of wartime. Members serving with the armed forces would receive a complete refund of their 1940 subscription, other members one-half of their annual fee.

In May, the British Empire Cricket Club came into existence and later that month the first game under wartime conditions was played between a British Empire XI, featuring mostly English county players, and Cambridge University, who managed their first victory since beating Hampshire in 1937. The London Counties XI also played its first match. Many service and civil defence organisation teams were being formed, their matches keeping up morale as well as raising funds for wartime charities. Although some county clubs had closed down for the duration, others also did arrange matches. Nottinghamshire played six at their Trent Bridge headquarters in 1940. On 7 September, the government ruled that cricketers taking part in matches in London must take cover during the period of an air-raid warning. This saw a match between Middlesex and a Lord's XI held up for quite some time. When it finally resumed, the right-arm fast-medium bowler Laurie Gray ended the game in dramatic fashion, taking four Lord's wickets in only seven balls to win the match. The 1940 cricket season ended without Lancashire's suggestion, of a regionalised county championship to include the Minor Counties, being taken up.

When the 1939–40 peacetime Rugby League competition was abandoned after the declaration of war, clubs faced the problem of what to do about supporters who had paid in advance for season tickets. Barrow resolved to give refunds, but would deduct for games already played. Oldham decided to keep all the money. 'We are up against it and must appeal to our members to make this sacrifice.' The Rugby Football League arranged a wartime competition based on two regional divisions – Yorkshire and Lancashire – with the winners of each playing a two-legged final to determine the overall champions. The minimum entrance fee was set at sixpence. As in soccer, clubs could use guest players, although there was the threat of industrial action when part-time players accustomed to receiving £4–£5 as a match fee were offered instead only 10s 'expenses'. This was later increased to £1. Clubs could also make an additional payment of 5s for away matches in Hull and Barrow, due to the extra travelling time needed to get there. Quite what Hull and Barrow players thought of that – their away games were obviously of equal inconvenience and came every other week not once or twice a season – is not clear.

On 2 March, the University Boat Race was held at Henley for the first time since the inaugural race in 1829. Rowing on the Thames in London with the riverbanks lined with thousands of spectators had been considered far too risky. Cambridge won the race by five lengths but no Blues were awarded. The 1940 event was decidedly 'unofficial'.

Nowhere, though, did the war disrupt sport as much as it did in soccer. The 1939–40 Football League programme was abandoned after only three matches, the Scottish League after five. The game's rulers' first reaction was not to make the same mistake as in 1914, when the Football League and the FA Cup had been allowed to continue for a whole season and everyone connected with the game had been denounced as both unpatriotic and unproductive. In November 1914, *The Times* had carried a letter from the historian A.H. Pollard:

'... Every club that employs a professional football player is bribing a much-needed recruit away from enlistment and every spectator who pays his gate money is contributing so much towards a German victory.'

In September 1939, the game closed down immediately. It had no choice. One of the government's first reactions after the declaration of war was to ban the assembly of large crowds. That meant that all forms of public entertainment had to be suspended immediately. So, unlike 1914, professional football could not carry on anyway. A few days after war had been declared, the government lifted its ban on sporting activities outside highly populated areas such as London, Birmingham and Manchester. On 9 September 1939, the first wartime football match took place behind closed doors at Loftus Road when Queen's Park Rangers put ten goals past a hastily recruited Army team. Just who were the eleven servicemen who were so roundly beaten, we shall never know; the Army team was not published for 'security reasons'.

On 25 September, the stipulation that matches could only be played between clubs no more than 50 miles apart was altered to allow games where the away team could be 'there and back in a day'. Three days earlier, attendances of up to 8,000 in evacuation areas and up to 15,000 in safer centres were allowed. There were stipulations, however. The limit of 8,000 could be no more than half the capacity of the stadium. The bigger grounds in the non-evacuation areas could admit up to 15,000 provided that tickets were sold in advance, an arrangement that soon proved impractical. Nevertheless, football supporters began to see their local grounds quickly re-opened, although had the local chief constable had his way, Birmingham would never have played a home match during the Second World War. When football was allowed to resume, police chief Cecil Moriarty was having none of it. In his opinion, the area around St Andrew's was a likely target for the Luftwaffe – as it turned out, he was right – and there would be the risk of serious loss of life if thousands of people were allowed to gather to watch football. The club did everything in their power to overturn his ruling and on 12 March 1940, Birmingham City Council passed a resolution asking the chief constable to reconsider. They argued that people who spent long hours working in munitions factories deserved some recreation and that included watching football at Birmingham. The matter was raised in the House of Commons, but Home Secretary Sir John Anderson declared that he could not intervene in such a local issue. A letter to the Birmingham *Sports Argus* accused Moriarty of 'killing people's Saturday afternoons', adding, 'He would change his views if he had to work in a factory for fifty or sixty hours a week.' Eventually, when it was pointed out that St Andrew's was the only football ground in Britain still closed, Chief Constable Moriarty and the eight Birmingham councillors who had backed him had no case. On 23 March, the ground reopened and there was an attendance of 13,241 to see Birmingham play Walsall in a Midland Division game, for by then the wartime regional competitions, with clubs fielding guest players from other clubs, were well under way. That would be the pattern of things until 1946 when the game resumed its peacetime format.

Frank Broome, the pre-war Aston Villa and England star, recalled:

'To be honest, the first wartime season of 1939–40 was very strange. It was quite enjoyable but a lot of the matches were played in a half-hearted manner. No one knew what was going to happen in the war. It wasn't easy to concentrate on football.'

Even in the first few weeks of the war, Mass Observation noted that the banning of competitive sports – and therefore the breaking of well-established routines – might have 'deep repercussions'. In 1940, Mass Observation reported:

'Sports like football have an absolute effect on the morale of the people and one Saturday afternoon of league matches could probably do more to affect people's spirits than the recent £50,000 Government poster campaign urging cheerfulness.'

The organisation could not find one pre-war football supporter who thought that the game should be suspended for the duration of the war. Perhaps more significantly, they found that only two per cent of people not interested in football in peacetime were against sport being played in time of war. Alas, in 1940 Mass Observation also found that 65 per cent of supporters who attended pre-war matches could not now get to football because of Saturday shift work in factories, travel restrictions and family obligations.

For those hoping for a wartime fortune, a new Unity Pools was formed combining Littlewood's, Vernon's, Cope's, Sherman's, Socapools, Bond's, Jervis and Screen's. The combined coupon saved paper and cut down on handling. The Edinburgh duo of Murphy's and Strang's had started the ball rolling two weeks earlier with their own combined coupon. In January 1940, a woman from Hull won a record Unity Pools dividend of £8,059 for an outlay of 1s 6d.

Sometimes, though, the pools had to be cancelled if there were insufficient matches. Bad weather had an inevitable effect on the first wartime season. York City, for instance, played no competitive matches from Christmas Day until 16 March. On 3 February, only one match in Britain could be played, when Bristol City lost 10–3 at Plymouth. Less than 900 people turned up to watch. The previous week, only seven of the scheduled fifty-nine games could be staged. One major problem for the clubs was that weather forecasts could not be published for fear of aiding the enemy, so there were no opportunities to warn supporters that matches were going to be cancelled.

By the beginning of March, clubs were asking for an extension to the season, not least so that a knockout competition, which they viewed as a potential money-spinner, could be fitted in. It was agreed that the season could run until June, and the preliminary rounds of the War Cup would begin on 13 April. An indication of how far behind the fixtures schedule had fallen came when the second round of the War Cup was played on 27 April, which would have been FA Cup Final day had there been no war. The sixty-four first-round matches – the ties were each played over two legs – had attracted almost half a million spectators. The Manchester derby alone was watched by a total of 43,000. Cup football was obviously what supporters wanted.

On 12 May, twelve British football coaches working in Holland escaped on one of the last boats to leave that country. The Phoney War had ended. The football season that had sometimes seemed almost as phoney as the war itself was also coming to its conclusion. The War Cup progressed to a Wembley Final – the stadium was now temporary home to hundreds of bewildered French and Belgian refugees who had fled Hitler's blitzkrieg into their countries – between West Ham United and Blackburn Rovers on 8 June. At half-time it was announced that there were 'six Dunkirk heroes' in the crowd. They sat in a special section with many of their wounded comrades who were dressed in hospital uniform of blue jacket, white shirt and red tie. The 42,000-crowd rose as one to give the soldiers a mighty roar of welcome. It was a far greater cheer even than that which had greeted the only goal of the game, scored by Sam Small of West Ham in the thirty-fourth minute. The Hammers' manager, Ted Fenton, later recalled the game as being about 'as hilarious as a wet Sunday in Cardiff'.

So the curtain came down on the first season of wartime football.

But did any of it really matter? On 31 May 1940, the *Daily Express* reported that football might be closed down until peace was restored 'due to team raising and transport problems'. In a Britain on the brink of being invaded, finding eleven half-decent footballers and a bus in which to transport them was hardly a priority.

Yet the game continued. As the second wartime football season got underway on 31 August 1940, the *Manchester Guardian* commented:

'When the time comes to write the history of this war, it may not pass unnoticed by the chronicler that, as the Battle of Britain developed, the Football League launched a season of competitive football. It is, at all events, no small act of temerity on the part of sixty-eight of the League's flock of eighty-eight to embark in this new wartime enterprise in circumstances obviously more difficult than those last winter and early spring.'

In the *Daily Express* Stanley Halsey reported:

'The entire Football League executive staff – secretary Fred Howarth and a 15-year-old office boy – wildly excited at being caught up in such vital football affairs – dashed from the Management Committee meeting in Manchester to League headquarters at Preston yesterday, to get busy with League plans for the coming season. Fortified by sandwiches, coffee and League decisions, they began the overtime job of ironing out the fix-your-own fixtures lists for next season, and tidying up the outstanding problems of wartime soccer.'

Two days later the Luftwaffe launched its most intensive attack on Britain. This was going to be an unusual sort of football season.

Watching the game as the Battle of Britain raged overhead could be a tiresome diversion, as well as a dangerous one. The Home Office ruled that play must be stopped whenever the air-raid alert sounded. Clubs attempted to counter this with a system of 'spotters'; even after the alert sounded, play would continue until the spotter on the roof of the stadium signalled the actual presence of enemy aircraft.

The government considered this too risky and refused its implementation, although it was eventually adopted. In the meantime, matches continued to be interrupted, occasionally for up to an hour. Players passed their time in various ways. Card games, singsongs, games of housey-housey, they all played their part in keeping footballers occupied while they waited for the all-clear. Some, however, got fed up and went home. When the referee went to round everyone up for a restart, often the teams could not be completed so the game was abandoned. Not unnaturally, many supporters also decided not to waste their Saturday afternoons hanging around in air-raid shelters waiting for the football to resume. For a club like Charlton Athletic, right underneath the air war, it was a particular problem. Attendances at The Valley dwindled to the low hundreds and the club was losing money every week. On 28 December 1940, their first round of fixtures completed, Charlton decided to close down for the rest of the season.

A clear indication of what was to follow had come as early as the opening day of the season. At The Dell, the League South game between Southampton and Brighton was held up for 30 minutes after an air-raid warning. The attendance of just over 1,000 reflected people's caution at attending football matches on the south coast when the Luftwaffe was likely to appear at any time. The biggest attendances of the day were in the north of England, with crowds of 5,000 at Liverpool and Newcastle, and 4,000 at Manchester City. In the south, no club rivalled that kind of support on the first day of a season that no one could guarantee would progress very far. The following Saturday, with only sixty seconds remaining at The Valley and the visitors, Millwall, leading Charlton Athletic 4–2, the air-raid warning siren sounded. The raid was a heavy one with shrapnel from nearby anti-aircraft guns falling on the stadium. The 1,500 spectators took cover and when the all-clear sounded, the game resumed and the final minute played out. A week later, Charlton's match at Brentford was interrupted after 65 minutes. Again the players resumed the game, this time before the remnants of a crowd that had numbered only 600 at kick-off.

League games were not the only form of football interrupted by the Battle of Britain. Ken Aston, who after the war made his name as an international referee, recalled the day he took charge of a services game with a steel helmet and a gas mask on his chest:

'I was a gunner on a gun site on a bomber station in 1940 when bomber stations were being heavily attacked by German aircraft, and a match had been arranged between the RAF personnel and the gunners who were operating the low-level-attack guns. There was this match, being played near my gun site. For that reason I was allowed to referee the game. In the middle of the game we hear a low droning sound. It was a day of low clouds. We look up at the aircraft and it is a JU–88. So I raced to my gun, whipped on my steel helmet and respirator that we had to wear – you never knew when there was going to be a gas attack – and manned the guns in refereeing kit. We had to abandon the game.'

It wasn't just the bombs that caused problems. The blackout was as much a nuisance to sportsmen as it was to the general public. But they coped. Southampton FC's coach driver, returning from a game at Cardiff, became lost in the blackout, then he hit a brick wall and finally the vehicle suffered a burst tyre. The players were forced to spend the night in the coach, not arriving back in Southampton until lunchtime the following day. The players of Wycombe Wanderers had probably the worst experience. After a Great Western Combination game at Slough, the Wycombe team had to walk the 15 miles back to High Wycombe.

In September 1940, the Germans released a propaganda photograph of a Heinkel He111 supposedly over the Surrey docks. In fact it was a fake, given away by the lack of the North Terrace cover at The Den, the home of Millwall, which had been roofed since 1938. Although The Den itself would escape bomb damage until later in the war, football grounds, too, were suffering. Matches at Brentford's Griffin Park were constantly interrupted by air-raid warnings; also in September 1940, a delayed-action bomb fell in Braemar Road, forcing the cancellation of the Bees' match against Chelsea

In August 1940, the government had decided that playing football at Southend Stadium was too risky, given Southend's position at the mouth of the Thames. With the continued presence of warships moored off its pier, the military garrison at Shoebury and the EKCO radio factory, Southend was declared a restricted zone and many of its children were evacuated. The stadium became a centre for training army officers and Southend United went to play at Chelmsford City's New Writtle Street ground. Unfortunately, no-one told Tottenham outside-right Tom Paton, who in December 1940 turned up expecting to play at Southend Stadium, only to discover that the home team had moved 20 miles down the road.

On 22 December 1940, Manchester United's ground suffered some damage but it was on 11 March the following year that the main stand was completely destroyed by one bomb, while another wrote off much of the terracing. The pitch was also rendered unplayable after it was badly scorched. United went to play their home games at City's Maine Road stadium in Moss Side – and would still be doing so until August 1949. Hull City's new ground on the Boothferry Road site had been earmarked as a multi-purpose sports complex as early as 1932. Progress was painstakingly slow and Hull finally looked forward to moving in for the 1940–41 season. The war put an end to their aspirations, not least because the Home Guard used the site and later on tanks were repaired on the pitch.

Bramall Lane, home to Sheffield United and also a venue for Yorkshire County Cricket Club, suffered badly during December 1940 when the steel-making city was the target of a massive air attack. Ten bombs fell on the ground itself, destroying a large section of the John Street Stand. The visitors' and referee's changing rooms, along with the club's medical room and about one-third of the ground's seating were lost. The roof of the Kop was also destroyed and there were two craters in front of the goal at the Bramall Lane End, and one at each end of the cricket pitch. The *Sheffield Telegraph* announced simply that the forthcoming game against Newcastle United had been cancelled – wartime censorship forbade the newspaper to explain that enemy action was to blame – and, indeed, there was no more football at Bramall Lane that season.

At Southampton, The Dell, only a mile from the docks, was hit several times, perhaps the most spectacular strike coming in November 1940 when a bomb fell on the pitch at the Milton Road End, creating an 18ft-wide crater. A culvert carrying a stream under the pitch was broken and

The Dell was soon under 3ft of water. It took a month before the culvert was repaired and the water subsided; in the meantime the Saints were forced to play all their matches away from home.

A German bomb hit Leicester City's Filbert Street ground on the frosty, moonlit night of 14 November 1940, when many British towns and cities were targeted in a massive attack by the Luftwaffe and the centre of Coventry, only 27 miles away, was almost destroyed. The damage to Filbert Street was mostly to the main stand, affecting the roof, seats, boardroom, gymnasium, kitchen and lavatories. The Leicester club, in dire financial straits even before the war started, was left with a repair bill estimated to be in the region of £15,000. A request for an FA loan to tide them over was met with a firm refusal. Did they not know there was a war on?

Chapter Seven

Women Doing Men's Work

'Equal pay for women doing war work is demanded'
Glasgow Trades Council

In May 1940, Sergeant Theresa Wallach of the Auxiliary Territorial Service (ATS) was fined 10s for exceeding the speed limit and £2 for driving at a dangerous speed on her motorcycle. Penge police court was told that on her way to take part in a speedway event at the Crystal Palace, Wallach had travelled at between 50 mph and 58mph in a 30mph zone. Wallach was already a well-known name. Five years earlier, together with another experienced motorcyclist, Florence Blenkiron, she had driven a motorcycle complete with sidecar and trailer from London to Cape Town, reportedly crossing the Sahara Desert without the aid of a compass. Upon the outbreak of war she became an army despatch rider and the court was told that if she lost her licence, she would not be able to do her work of national importance.

For most women, however, the war meant taking over civilian jobs normally done by men. The same month that Theresa Wallach was admonished for exceeding the speed limit while in army uniform, the local secretary of the Passenger Section of the Transport and General Workers' Union told the *Staffordshire Sentinel* that conductresses would soon be introduced on bus services run by Potteries Motor Transport (PMT). So far, 138 men employed by PMT had joined the armed forces and girls were already being registered to take their places. A national agreement had been negotiated between bus companies and union representatives for conductresses to be employed for the duration of the war and in principal towns and cities throughout the country some 4,000 girls – the newspaper always referred to them as 'girls' even though some must surely have been mature women – were already working in that role. The girls collecting bus fares for PMT would wear 'a smart uniform consisting of blue peaked cap with a soft crown, reefer jacket decorated with buttons bearing the company crest, blue knee-length skirts and dark stockings'.

More important than their uniform was the fact that they would receive the same pay as conductors, their male counterparts. An industrial court had considered the question of female labour in this particular industry and it had been decided that while no conductresses under the age of 18 would be employed, the wages of the rest would be on the basis of equal pay for equal employment. It was, of course, not just bus conductresses who felt they deserved to be paid the same. Throughout industry it was a thorny issue that refused to go away as more and more women found themselves doing 'man's work'.

In January 1940, at a meeting of many leading women's organisations in London, discrepancies between the wages and conditions of men and women engaged on national defence work were condemned. The meeting called on the government for 'adequate and equal pay for men and women'. The same month, Hartlepool's Trade Council included equal pay for women among a list it wanted the Trades' Union Congress to press the government for. Its other demands included a minimum wage of £4 for a 40-hour week for all adult workers, abolition of the Means Test for recipients of benefits, adequate increments in unemployment pay, increased old-age pensions, and that blind persons received 27s 6d per week plus the increase in the cost of living.

In March, the Central Council of the National Union of Women Teachers (NUWT) sent a letter to the government, urging that teachers' salaries be increased to meet the rising cost of living. The union added that 'while in no way relinquishing the claim that there should be equal pay for men and women teachers of the same professional status [the NUWT] is of the opinion that as an interim step there should be an immediate and adequate bonus payment to all teachers alike, irrespective of sex, scale, or teaching experience'.

While many female schoolteachers are still waiting for the gender gap to close, in May 1940 it was announced that agreement had been reached between employers and trade unions to allow more women to be brought into the engineering industry for the period of the war. Women who satisfied certain standards could earn the same rate and bonus payable to men, although their employment was to be regarded as only temporary – this would not affect the permanent status of women already working in industry – and only at the end of thirty-two weeks' employment, if they could show that without additional help or supervision they were able to carry out the work of the men they replaced, would they receive the basic rate and national bonus appropriate to men. Many employers – included Rolls-Royce at its Hillington, Glasgow, factory where Merlin aero-engines were produced – circumvented the issue for some time, and overall women's pay remained on average 53 per cent of the pay of the men they replaced. Semi-skilled and unskilled work was designated as 'women's jobs' exempt from equal pay negotiations. Women were still being discriminated against in other areas. The 1939 Personal Injuries (Civilians) Scheme paid men 21s per week in settlement whereas women received only 14s a week, despite the fact that they too worked as ambulance drivers, fire-watchers, air-raid wardens, in first-aid parties and as messengers during the Blitz. It would be 1943 before the government relented and paid women the same settlement as men.

In 1940, women were still not being called-up. Just as in the First World War, they had volunteered for essential work so that men might be released to join the armed forces. As war loomed in 1939, there were campaigns reminding women that they may well have to volunteer again, but after the outbreak of war, and particularly after the fall of France when British troops became fully engaged with the enemy, it was clear that this time volunteering was not going to meet the demands of wartime production. In November 1940, Sir William Beveridge reported to the government, in secret, that the conscription of women into either the services (although not under fire), Civil Defence, and especially into wartime industrial production was going to be unavoidable. Their labour would be needed not only to collect bus fares, and even to drive buses, ambulances and fire engines, but also to take on skilled work in armaments and aeroplane factories, shipyards and the like. In December 1941, the National Service Act (no 2) made the conscription of women legal and by mid-1943 almost 90 per cent of single women and 80 per cent of married women were employed in essential work for the war effort. In 1940, there were only fourteen state-funded nurseries where working women could leave their children. Once women were conscripted, that had to change and by the war's end there were 1,345 such nurseries.

While they fought the battle to bring women's pay into line with that of the men who they, temporarily at least, replaced, it was only one of the issues that occupied trades' unions in 1940. Although wholly sympathetic – 'equal pay for women doing war work is demanded' – Glasgow Trades' Council was in more militant mood. In April, at the Scottish Trades' Union Congress, it proclaimed that the war was 'an imperialist one' and called upon the movement to take immediate action to stop it. Holding similar views, the Scottish Brassmoulders' Union called upon German workers suffering under Hitler to struggle against the Nazi government, although quite how they were going to do that while in the iron grip of such a totalitarian regime was not explored. Meanwhile, Sir Walter Citrine, the general secretary of the Trades' Union Council (TUC) and president of the International Federation of Trades' Unions, together with other TUC leaders came in for criticism over their recent visit to Finland where 'the object of the campaign being conducted by Finnish generals, with the fullest sympathy and support of the British Government, is to extend the present war against the Soviet Union'. In May, as Hitler launched his offensive on France and the Low Countries, the *Daily Worker*, the newspaper of organised Communism in Britain, described the war effort as 'the Anglo–French imperialist war machine'. Until the Soviet Union entered the war in 1941, British Communists would show surprisingly little enthusiasm for a war against Fascism.

On 10 July 1940, the government introduced Defence Regulation 58AA that invested in the Minister of Labour the power to ban strikes and lockouts, and force compulsory arbitration. Order 1305 allowed the Minister of Labour and National Service, Ernest Bevin, one of the great names of the Trades' Union movement, to refer any dispute to existing arbitration structures or to the National Arbitration Tribunal. Either alternative was to be binding. The chief industrial commissioner for the Ministry of Labour, Frederick William Leggett, had reservations. 'The Order has a substantial deterrent effect but it is an instrument which would probably be shown to be useless if any considerable body of workpeople chose to defy it.' It was a well-considered point. Although no trade union called an official strike during the war, there were many short, local ones, especially in coalmines, shipyards and munitions factories. In January 1942, the Ministry of Labour would prosecute 1,050 Kent miners for contravening Order 1305 during a dispute over the level of allowances for working difficult seams. Three local union officials would be imprisoned, men working difficult seams each fined £3, and 1,000 other miners fined £1 each. The strike, at Betteshanger Colliery, continued and other pits came out in sympathy. In February, the Home Secretary scrapped the prison sentences and by May only nine miners had paid their fines. Most fines were never paid.

Yet if at times the workers were restless and dissatisfied with their lot, an appearance by the king and queen at a factory or shipyard was always met with universal approval. Royal visits were regularly reported throughout 1940. The purpose of them varied, from meeting victims of the Blitz and viewing the destruction, to talking to workers at factories doing work of national importance. From ruined areas in places like Liverpool, Manchester, Hull and, of course, London, especially the East End, to shipyards on Tyneside and at Greenock, armaments factories in Birmingham, Nottingham and Derby, and at Kilmarnock and Paisley, the visits were never announced in advance but were soon surrounded by cheering crowds. On 18 April, the royal couple visited Birmingham. The *Birmingham Mail* reported:

'The king and queen arrived at Small Heath station at 10.10 a.m., and as if by magic a large crowd gathered outside to greet them. How they got to know about the Royal visit is a mystery, for it had been kept an official secret.'

Among the places they visited were the BSA works and the Wolseley Motors factory where 14-year-old George Tattin, 'at 4ft 3ins tall, a Tom Thumb of a lad', told the queen that he had worked there as a riveter for the past nine months 'and that he was very happy about it. He looked as though he was still happy when she bestowed upon him a characteristic smile'. Everywhere the royal couple went they were 'cut off and engulfed by the surging excited hundreds of employees who could not be kept in check ... employees completely surrounded the king and queen who smilingly accepted this astonishing demonstration of loyalty such as seldom been seen in Birmingham before'.

On Thursday, 8 August 1940, the people of Derby awoke to learn that they had special visitors; the king and queen were coming to town. The fact that the royal couple was to tour Rolls-Royce – where the Merlin engines that powered Britain's hopes in the Battle of Britain were manufactured – meant that their visit had to remain secret until the last possible moment. But word somehow got out and thousands were waiting at the LMS station when King George VI and Queen Elizabeth arrived. The king, wearing the uniform of colonel-in-chief of the Grenadier Guards, was told by Derby's mayor, Alderman Arthur Neal, 'You will find your citizens here as loyal as any in the British Empire.' After inspecting Indian mounted troops stationed at Osmaston polo grounds, the king and queen walked through the Rolls-Royce factory where journalists and photographers were excluded from the experimental department. Then, after meeting First World War VC Charles Stone, stroking the factory cat and appearing on a balcony to wave to workers, they returned to the town's main railway station, leaving Derby to get on with its war.

Chapter Eight

'Let Us Go Forward Together ...'

'... We cannot go on as we are. There must be a change.'
Leo Amery MP

On 10 May 1940, meeting in Bournemouth, the Labour Party executive unanimously resolved to 'take their share of responsibility as a full partner in a new government under a new Prime Minister who would command the confidence of the nation'. Directly after the vote was taken, the Labour leader, Clement Attlee, and his deputy, Arthur Greenwood, left for London and 10 Downing Street. The Labour executive had earlier declared that 'in view of the latest abominable aggressions by Hitler, while firmly convinced that a drastic reconstruction of the government is vital and urgent in order to win the war, reaffirms its determination to do its utmost to achieve victory, and calls upon all its members to devote all their energies to this end and to stand firmly united through whatever trials and sacrifices may lie ahead'. So, for the moment, party politics were to be set aside.

The previous day, the Liberal Party leader, Sir Archibald Sinclair, had issued a statement:

'Recent events have proved the necessity for a prompt and radical reconstruction of the British government, but the opening of the first critical battle in the West is not the moment. The German attack aimed at Britain and France has been launched with characteristic disregard of the rights and freedoms of small nations. The assault must be broken by the skill and courage of the fighting forces of the Allies, back in this, as in other countries, by the firm will of a united people.'

After he had been informed of the Labour Party's decision, Neville Chamberlain, the Conservative prime minister, summoned the War

Cabinet and told them of his decision to resign. Thirty minutes later, the rest of his ministers joined them in the Cabinet Room. It was to be their last meeting with Chamberlain as their chairman. Hardly had they left Downing Street when Chamberlain and his Parliamentary Private Secretary, Lord Dunglass (who, as Sir Alec Douglas-Home, would become Britain's prime minister for a year from 1963) left too, to be driven to Buckingham Palace. As they went Chamberlain raised his hat in response to the cheers of several hundred people who had stopped to temporarily line his route. At the Palace, Chamberlain handed his resignation to the king. Shortly afterwards Winston Churchill, who earlier in the day had been given a great ovation in Downing Street, was driven to the Palace where he accepted the king's invitation to become prime minister. Churchill remained at the Palace for 40 minutes before undertaking his 'walk with destiny'. A National Government of all parties was about to be formed.

Chamberlain's decision to resign had become inevitable. In times of peace he may well have weathered the storm that had engulfed him. In war, when national unity was vital, he had, as the London correspondent of *The Scotsman* put it, 'rightly declined to be an obstacle to the attainment of that end'. Prime Minister since 1937, the following year he had, along with France and Italy, signed the Munich Agreement that relinquished the Sudetenland, a region of Czechoslovakia populated mainly by German speakers, to the Nazis. The 'appeasement' would follow Chamberlain to his grave. Yet despite that, in early April 1940, according to a poll, he still enjoyed the approval of almost 60 per cent of the British people. But on 9 April, Germany invaded Norway and on 26 April, the War Cabinet ordered the British troops, who had arrived too late and in too small a number to defend the Norwegians, to withdraw instead.

Chamberlain's opponents decided to use the adjournment debate for the Whitsun recess as a challenge to his leadership. What became known as the 'Norway Debate' opened on 7 May and lasted for two days. At the debate got under way, the public were watching the first cinema newsreel film of Royal Navy ships in action off Narvik, and British soldiers in Norway. As always, the tone of the British Pathé voiceover was upbeat. In the House of Commons, however, the mood was anything but. Chamberlain's whole conduct of the war was being questioned, but especially what had happened in Norway was the point. Chamberlain had already angered Lieutenant-Colonel Leo Amery, the Conservative

MP for Birmingham Sparkbrook, when, on 2 September 1939, the prime minister had hinted that Britain might not declare war on Germany immediately, even if it did invade Poland. Amery felt that Chamberlain was out of touch with public opinion. Now he took issue with him over Norway, telling the House:

'We had only this inadequate little force, without transports, of which the Prime Minister has told us, in readiness to occupy Norwegian western ports if there were German action against southern Norway. There was no plan to meet the contingency that Germany might seize the western ports as well or to meet any really serious attack by Germany upon Norway ... We cannot go on as we are. There must be a change. First and foremost, it must be a change in the system and structure of our governmental machine. This is war, not peace. The essence of peacetime democratic government is discussion, conference and agreement; the Cabinet is in a sense a miniature Parliament. The main aim is agreement, the widest possible measure of agreement. To secure that it is necessary to compromise, to postpone, to rediscuss. Under those conditions there are no far-reaching plans for sudden action. It is a good thing to let policies develop as you go along and get people educated by circumstances. That may or may not be ideal in peace. It is impossible in war. In war the first essential is planning ahead. The next essential is swift, decisive action ... Surely, for the government of the last ten years to have bred a band of warrior statesmen would have been little short of a miracle. We have waited for eight months, and the miracle has not come to pass. Can we afford to wait any longer?'

Amery concluded his speech:

'Somehow or other we must get into the Government men who can match our enemies in fighting spirit, in daring, in resolution and in thirst for victory. Some 300 years ago, when this House found that its troops were being beaten again and again by the dash and daring of the Cavaliers, by Prince Rupert's cavalry, Oliver Cromwell spoke to John Hampden. In one of his speeches he recounted what he said. It was this ... "Your troops are most of them old, decayed serving men and tapsters and such kind of fellows ... You must get men of a spirit that are likely to go as far as they will go, or you will be beaten still." It may not be easy to find these men. They can be found only by trial and by ruthlessly discarding all who fail and have their failings discovered. We are fighting today for our life, for our liberty, for our all; we cannot go on being led as we are. I have quoted certain words of Oliver Cromwell. I will quote certain other words. I do it with great reluctance, because I am speaking of those who are old friends and associates of mine, but they are words, which, I think, are applicable to the present situation. This is what Cromwell said to the Long Parliament when he thought it was no longer fit to conduct the affairs of the nation: "You have sat too long here for any good you have been doing. Depart, I say, and let us have done with you. In the name of God, go.'"

The Chamberlain government's notional majority was 213, but 41 of its usual supporters, including 29 Conservatives, voted with the Opposition, while a further 60 Tory MPs abstained. The government had won the motion by 281 votes to 200, but the reduced majority was a crushing blow to Chamberlain's authority. As he left the chamber there were cries of 'Go!'

The *Daily Herald*'s political correspondent, Maurice Webb, commented:

'Sweeping reconstruction of the government involving the possible resignation of Mr Chamberlain is now widely regarded as inevitable in the near future ... the Prime Minister's speech yesterday was regarded in every responsible quarter as that of a losing man. It was described to me as "his obituary notice". It has depressed and dismayed even the most unquestioning loyalists. And in everyone else it has aroused undisguised apprehension. The one topic among MPs of all parties last night was the Prime Minister's obvious loss of his customary self assurance and confidence.'

The Birmingham *Evening Despatch* said:

'It is a poor consolation to boast of the skilful way in which withdrawal from Norway was effected. The real point is that our soldiers ought not to have been placed in so precarious a position that their withdrawal was necessary … Where Mr Chamberlain errs is in so blandly minimising the seriousness of the setback and the gravity of its effect on world opinion. His inevitable complacency is a dangerous drug impeding our war effort.'

A new man was needed to bring Parliament together, and so Winston Churchill became Britain's prime minister, although in some ways almost through default. The foreign secretary, Lord Halifax, had, in many people's eyes, been the obvious choice to succeed Chamberlain but Halifax ruled himself out because he feared the consequences of having to lead the war effort from the House of Lords. George VI preferred Halifax but when the Labour Party and Liberal Party had voted to join the National Government, they stated that they preferred Churchill who, despite many flaws, had always shown unstinting opposition to Hitler. Parliament now realised that he was the man to lead Britain in her most desperate hour. On 13 May, Churchill met his Cabinet, telling them, 'I have nothing to offer but blood, toil, tears and sweat.' Later that day, facing the House of Commons for the time as prime minister, he repeated that phrase when he asked for a vote of confidence in his new all-party government. 'At this time I feel entitled to claim the aid of all, and I say, "come then, let us go forward together with our united strength."'

On 3 October 1940, Neville Chamberlain resigned from the government altogether. He was suffering from terminal bowel cancer. The *Yorkshire Post* commented:

'He has been criticised for not understanding that it was never possible of achievement, given the character, doctrines and plans of the bandits of Europe with whom he had to deal. But he did what he could in ways that he believed best; and the effort, though foredoomed to failure, had one important result for the moral credit of Britain. It was proof to the world, including many in the now enemy countries, that Britain's aim was peace, a peace reasonable and just for all.'

Neville Chamberlain died on 9 November 1940, aged 71.

Chapter Nine

A Seething Tide of Humanity

'They looked lost, absolutely lost. It made us realise that we weren't invincible.'

Alf Turner

Writing in the *Portsmouth Evening News* on Monday, 7 October 1940, K. Gilson said:

'October now, and a year ago we were saying, well, that's a month of war gone ... and we had hardly heard or seen anything of it, the sirens were a novelty, sounded a time or two for practice but rarely for the real thing. Those days have gone: they were comparatively peaceful; France was our supposedly strong ally ... her Empire at least will rally and remain so – fighting was very far away, and not serious, blitzkriegs something that looked all right on paper but ... Then, month after month, the situation looked more and more desperate, but still the war did not touch us personally until just before Dunkirk, and then we began to realise ...'

'Dunkirk' – before May 1940 the name meant little, if anything, to anyone in Britain. It was simply the name of a French port that most people had never visited and were never likely to, and nothing more. It certainly had nothing to do with the present conflict. Indeed, on the first day of the year, some four months after war had been declared, the Gibson Rankine Line was still advertising its regular service from Grangemouth to Dunkirk and Rotterdam. Those interested in particulars of sailings and freight rates were invited to contact the company's offices in Glasgow or Leith. If newspapers mentioned Dunkirk in the context of war, it was only to look back to January 1915 and mark the twenty-fifth anniversary of an attempted air-raid on England when sixteen German aircraft were forced to turn back because of bad weather over the English Channel and were last seen 'steering in the direction of Dunkirk'.

On Friday, 10 May 1940, Gibson Rankine was still offering to take passengers and freight from Grangemouth to Dunkirk and Rotterdam. Yet, that same day, British newspapers were reporting that William C. Bullitt, the US ambassador in Paris, had telephoned Washington to report that the Luftwaffe had bombed Calais and Dunkirk. In fact several French towns had been bombed and, according to reports from the British Embassy in Paris, sixteen people had been killed and thirty injured, most of them civilians. It was the start of Hitler's invasion of France and the Low Countries. The war had taken a huge turn. That day, German paratroopers captured key bridges in the Netherlands and Belgium before ground troops crossed over the Dutch and Belgian borders, neatly avoiding the Maginot Line, the series of fortifications that France had constructed along her own border with Germany.

The British Expeditionary Force that had been sent to France in September 1939 and which now numbered ten divisions in three corps under the command of Lord Gort, advanced from the Belgian border towards positions along the River Dyle where they came into contact with the enemy. Four days later, after the French and Belgians had failed to hold their positions on the British flanks, the BEF was ordered to begin a fighting withdrawal along the River Scheldt. In the Netherlands, the game was already up: the military had surrendered to Germany; Queen Wilhelmina and her government were on their way to London.

By the evening of 12 May, the Germans were pouring over the Belgian border into France. They next day they crossed the River Meuse, broke through French defences, then turned north-west towards the English Channel. In Paris on 17 May, Churchill learned that the French Army had no strategic reserves. Two days later General Gaston Billotte, commander of the French First Army, informed Lord Gort that France had no troops between the Germans and the sea. Although the French did not yet know it, Gort then immediately began to plan the evacuation of more than one-third of a million troops to England. Dunkirk, surrounded by marshes and with long, sandy beaches and good port facilities, offered the best embarkation point. The withdrawal to the coast began. On 20 May, at Churchill's suggestion, the Admiralty began plans for every kind of small vessel to be made ready to proceed to the French coast in order to take off the huge army that was gathering there. Back in Britain on 21 May, astonishingly, Gibson Rankine was still advertising its service from Grangemouth to Dunkirk and Rotterdam, even though the first German tanks had arrived on the southern outskirts of the Dutch city nine days earlier, and Dunkirk was about to become the scene of the biggest military evacuation in history.

On 28 May, King Leopold III of Belgium, with his government already in exile in Paris, took the only option realistically open to him – the unconditional surrender of his country to Germany. In the House of Commons, Churchill defended Leopold's decision even though it made the BEF's attempt to reach Dunkirk more precarious still. It left British forces to the east of Dunkirk wide open to attack and several divisions were rushed to defend the gap. Leopold, meanwhile, refused to leave his country and would spend the war as a prisoner of the Nazis, albeit in the confines of his palace.

For one British civilian the Germans' lightning swoop into Belgium heralded days of danger and hair-raising adventure. Dundonald Jackson's home was in Derby, but in May 1940 he was a Rolls-Royce service engineer working in Belgium. On the day of the German invasion, he waited until nightfall before making a dash for safety with his wife and personal assistant. Along the road leading to the Belgian coast they passed hundreds of British soldiers moving up to the front line. On one occasion they were forced to abandon their car and take refuge in a ditch as a German fighter aircraft machine-gunned the road. Eventually they were able to board a Belgian steamer jammed full of refugees. Again they were strafed by the Luftwaffe. After a perilous journey across the Channel they landed in England and made their way home to a town still trying to come to terms with the fact that the invasion of Britain was now a very real possibility.

Dunkirk was now the focus of civilians back home, even those who had never wished to take advantage of the Gibson Rankine Line's regular sailings there. 'Dunkirk not yet menaced,' said the *Derby Evening Telegraph* headline, as late as 29 May. In an agency report, the paper told its readers:

'It was learned in authoritative circles in London today that the BEF is still intact and together. They have withdrawn some miles towards the coast but it is impossible to say where they are at the present time. There seems, however, little doubt that they have not lost their cohesion ...'

One week later Derby's main railway station saw the arrival of 6,000 men, some of the remnants of the BEF, still wearing the uniforms in which they had been plucked out of the sea off the French port whose name would become one of the most powerful symbols of the Second World War. Alf Turner, an engineer at Rolls-Royce, remembered seeing many of the survivors standing in London Road. 'They looked lost, absolutely lost. It made us realise that we weren't invincible.'

Admiral Bertram Ramsey, who had come out of retirement in 1939, was directing the evacuation from deep under the White Cliffs of Dover. He and his staff worked from a room that had once housed a dynamo to generate electricity. Hence the name of the operation that he was conducting. Operation Dynamo took until 4 June to be completed. When it was done, some 338,000 Allied troops – 198,000 of them British; 140,000 French and Belgian – had been evacuated. But the BEF had lost more than 68,000 of its men – killed, wounded or taken prisoner – during the short and unsuccessful battle to save France, while almost all its tanks, other vehicles and heavy guns had been abandoned to the Germans.

Six Royal Navy destroyers were sunk during the operation that was carried out under round-the-clock air attacks and shore-based German artillery bombardment, but destroyers, troopships and landing craft still rescued an estimated two-thirds of those saved. The civilian ships that Churchill had suggested be made ready were also vital. The Royal Navy chartered some but others were simply commandeered. They numbered over 700 and included old sailing boats, rowing boats, river launches, pleasure steamers, commercial barges, fishing boats and fire boats. None of them were built for war and many had never before been to sea. Some owners chose to the sail their boats to France themselves rather than hand them over. Of the 220 vessels lost during the evacuation, more than 100 were the 'Little Ships'.

Significant among British losses on land was the 51st Highland Division that had been placed under French command. In his war diary, Captain Robert Macrae recorded:

'The French Corps, under whom we had been, now surrendered and left the 51 Div to carry on ... However we never got further than the start line as the Bde Major [brigade major] came up and said that it was "all over" and the 51 Div. had capitulated. The men were ordered to lay down their arms and collect what food and kit they could. All officers remained with their men until they were marched off by the Germans into captivity.'

That was a particularly bitter blow but if the whole BEF had been captured, not only would it have meant the loss of almost the entire number of Britain's trained troops able to continue the war, it would also have been a huge blow to civilian morale. As it was, the fall of France and the threat of invasion now brought the inevitable rumours. A local parish council called upon Derbyshire's chief constable to investigate reports that aliens in the village had been passing information to the Germans. The Rolls-Royce Thrift Society found it necessary to post notices denying a rumour that the government would confiscate any cash left in their accounts by 1 June, while a meeting of 500 men from Derby's Carriage and Wagon Works heard that they faced redundancy because after the fall of Norway there was a shortage of timber. Even going to the pictures was affected. Derby Town Council refused to allow cinemas to open on Sundays because staff shortages meant that safety regulations could not be implemented. On 31 May, workman had begun taking down road signs in towns and cities, nameplates on railway stations were removed and destination boards on buses disappeared. Bus conductors were ordered not to call out the names of stops.

The 'Dunkirk spirit' might yet see the nation through the Blitz that was soon to come, but when Churchill spoke to the House of Commons on 4 June, his 'We shall fight them on the beaches ... we will never surrender ...' speech, now regarded as perhaps the most rousing address of the entire war, also contained the warning that the successful evacuation 'must not blind us to the fact that what has happened in France and Belgium is a colossal military disaster'.

Britain, though, was already under no illusion that this was a backs-to-the-wall situation. The progress of the fighting in France and the retreat to Dunkirk had been reported in detail in newspapers. The *Liverpool Echo* said that the BEF was 'fighting like hell'. The *Newcastle Evening Chronicle* told readers that gunfire had been heard off the south-east coast 'coming apparently from the direction of Calais or Dunkirk ... there were also heavy detonations thought to be bomb explosions'.

The censors spared the British public very little in the way of graphic detail. In the *Daily Herald*, Wallace King, the paper's former Berlin correspondent, wrote an article entitled 'The Road From Brussels' in which he described 'a seething tide of humanity pouring in from all districts east and south of the city. They were ragged, hungry, frightened and tired'. They told King how they had been machine-gunned in cold blood, and he wrote of 'more tales of terror and barbarity ...' One woman told of how she had been swept along by the stream of fleeing refugees and had been forced to leave the bodies of her four children, all killed by German bullets, where they had fallen.

As K. Gilson was to write, '... and then we began to realise ...'

Water dribbles from a frozen tap in mid-Wales during the harsh winter of 1940. (*National Library of Wales/Geoff Charles*)

Police officers at Welshpool explain about gas masks. The van in the background was used as a testing chamber for the masks. (*National Library of Wales / Geoff Charles*)

Blackout curtains on an F.W. Woolworth store in Biggin Street, Dover, Kent, February 1940. (*Daily Express / Hulton Archive / Getty Images*)

Advertisement for shields to dim vehicle headlights during the blackout. (*Author's collection*)

Advice for staying safe during the blackout. (*Author's collection*)

Welsh RAF personnel enjoy front-row seats at Wembley for the England-Wales football unofficial wartime international in April 1940. (*Author's collection*)

Sergeant Theresa Wallach (right), an 'adventure motorcyclist' who was fined for speeding in Surrey in May 1940, became an ATS recruitment star. (*Author's collection*)

A convoy driven by ATS personnel gets ready to set out in a snowy Midlands. (*Author's collection*)

The war provided women with many opportunities to take on unfamiliar roles. These two are learning the secrets of a bus. Note the blacked-out headlamps. (*Author's collection*)

Women workers pictured at a munitions factory in the north of England. (*Illustrated London News*)

Helping on the Home Front: troops from a cavalry remount division are put to work on the land, ploughing a Midlands field. (*Author's collection*)

Men of RAF Balloon Command make the best of it as they await the bombing. (*Author's collection*)

The iconic figure of 1940: Prime
Minister Winston Churchill.
(*Illustrated London News*)

Troops returning from Dunkirk
load their equipment at Derby's
main railway station in June
1940. (*Author's collection*)

King George VI inspects Indian troops who were evacuated from Dunkirk. (*Author's collection*)

WVS members in Wales proudly display the aluminium pots and pans they have collected in response to Lord Beaverbrook's appeal. (*National Library of Wales/Geoff Charles*)

RAF Fighter Command crews await the next order to 'Scramble!' (*Illustrated London News*)

Home Guard recruits keeping fit at a bomb-damaged football ground in August 1940. (*Author's collection*)

Llahndyssil Home Guard pictured after a church parade in September 1940. Some of the men are wearing medals awarded during the First World War. (*National Library of Wales / Geoff Charles*)

Home Guard volunteers removing road signs in Kent during the invasion scare in September 1940. (*Doyle Collection*)

The Home Guard were a target for advertisers. (*Author's collection*)

Anderson shelters in gardens at Oldknow Road, Small Heath, Birmingham. (*The Library of Birmingham WK/B11/4875*)

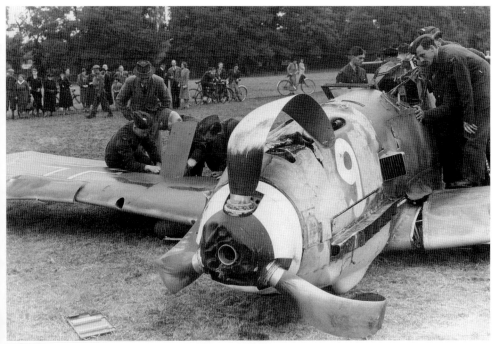

RAF Maintenance Unit personnel examine the wreckage of a Messerschmitt BF 109E-1 flown by Oberleutnant Karl Fischer that was shot down and crash landed near Queen Anne's Gate in Windsor Great Park on 30 September 1940. (*Fox Photos/Hulton Archive/Getty Images*)

A police officer notes damage to a house in the Midlands after a lone bomber struck in June 1940. (*Author's collection*)

Children evacuated from Birmingham arriving at Ripley railway station in Derbyshire on 15 November 1940. (*Staff/Mirrorpix/Getty Images*)

Soldiers march past the ruins of buildings on Broadgate, Coventry, on 16 November 1940. The Owen Owen department store can be seen in the distance. (*Imperial War Musuem*)

Residents survey bomb-damaged houses at Ivydale Avenue, Sheldon, Birmingham. (*The Library of Birmingham WK/B11/4861*)

Luftwaffe map of targets in Liverpool. November 1940. (*Liverpool Record Office*)

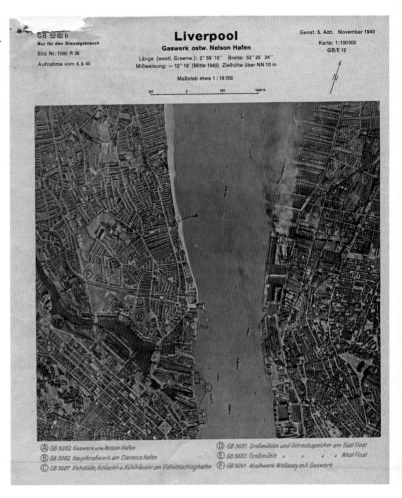

Armband issued to employees at the *Hull Daily Mail* in 1940, allowing them to reach work through bomb-damaged areas closed to the general public. (*Author's collection*)

In September 1940 a German bomber on its way to Merseyside dumped a bomb over mid-Wales. These children are showing bits of bomb casing to a gamekeeper. (*National Library of Wales/Geoff Charles*)

Smoke rises from fires in Surrey docks, following the first German air raid of the London Blitz, 7 September 1940. (*Keystone/Hulton Archive/Getty Images*)

An unexploded incendiary bomb found in a Midlands field in September 1940. (*Author's collection*)

Fighting spirit: Wally's barber's shop in St Martin Street displays defiant signs in November 1940 after losing its windows during the London blitz. (*Fox Photos/Getty Images*)

Internationally acclaimed dancer 27-year-old Ena Squire-Brown leaves her bombed home for St George's Church in Forest Hill, to marry Flying Officer J.C. Martin on 5 November 1940. (*Keystone-France/Gamma-Keystone via Getty Images*)

Chapter Ten

Bewilderment in Shipping Circles

'What were the reasons which caused him to withhold for five weeks
the news as to the sinking?'

Lieutenant-Colonel Sir Assheton Pownall MP

On 17 June 1940, 4,000 men, women and children lost their lives when
SS *Lancastria* was sunk off the French port of Saint-Nazaire. It would
prove to be the largest loss of life from a single engagement for British
forces in the entire war and the largest loss of life in British maritime
history. Yet it was the one tragedy surrounding Dunkirk about which the
British at home were initially kept in ignorance.

Even after the evacuation had been completed there were still an
estimated 150,000 British military personnel in France. When it
became apparent that the new French prime minister, Marshal Henri
Petain, was going to agree an armistice with Germany – it was signed
on 22 June and went into effect at midnight three days later – another
evacuation was quickly organised. The Cunard liner *Lancastria* was used
as a troopship and set sail for England laden with far more than her
peacetime capacity of 1,785 passengers. Thousands of army personnel
from a variety of units, together with 800 RAF maintenance crew in the
lower hold and hundreds of civilian refugees were wedged into the ship.
In the rush to embark, no accurate records were kept but it is estimated
that at least 4,000 people – some figures put that as high as 5,800 –
were killed. Survivors numbered 2,077. At 3.48pm, the *Lancastria* was
attacked in the Loire estuary by Junkers Ju 88 aircraft. She was hit three
times and listed first to starboard and then to port before a fourth bomb
fell straight down her smokestack. It detonated in the engine room and
twenty minutes later, the ship sank.

The government's immediate response to the disaster was to try to
impose a news blackout. It could not be supressed indefinitely, though.

On 25 July, five weeks after the sinking, the story broke in Northern Ireland when the *Northern Whig* newspaper repeated a report from the previous day's *New York Sun* that the *Lancastria* had gone down in a matter of minutes and that of 6,000 British troops on board 'only 600 were lost despite the lifeboats and rafts being machine-gunned'. The following day, the *Daily Herald* repeated the *New York Sun*'s story, although revising the loss of life to '500 men'. Within a day the story was everywhere. The *Liverpool Evening Express* reported on Wilfred Hyde of Southport, a purser who had not only survived the *Lancastria* sinking but also that of the SS *Counsellor* that had struck a mine on 8 March 1940. Mr Hyde told the *Evening Express* that he had simply walked off the *Lancastria* as she was sinking and had spent some time in the water. As he was leaving the ship, a barrel rolled overboard and some British soldiers, who were removing their outer clothing before swimming clear, began to sing *Roll Out The Barrel*. Another survivor from Southport was 20-year-old Aircraftman Alec Threlfall who had been in France for only six weeks. He had clung on to the side of a crowded lifeboat until a French tanker picked him up.

The delay in reporting the disaster was met with huge criticism.

On 31 July, the Minister of Information, Duff Cooper, came under fire in the House of Commons. Manny Shinwell, the Labour MP for Seaham Harbour, asked Cooper whether he could explain why a request by the *Journal of Commerce*, submitted on 24 June, to publish a paragraph on the sinking of the steamship *Lancastria* had been refused; and why, although the minister had promised to make a report on 2 July, no report had appeared until 24 July when the American Press had disclosed the facts; and was he aware that the attitude of the Ministry of Information has caused bewilderment in Liverpool and in shipping circles, where the facts had been known three days after the event?

Cooper replied that news of the bombing and sinking of the *Lancastria* had been withheld because she was engaged in a military operation and it had been clear from German wireless announcements that the enemy had been totally unaware of the identity of the ship that they had just sunk. It was contrary to the government's general policy, he said, to announce the loss of an individual ship but the number and total tonnage were given in weekly statements and the tonnage of the *Lancastria* was given in the statement for 2 July. The policy was well known and he could not understand why, on this occasion, 'bewilderment should have been caused in Liverpool and in shipping circles'.

Edgar Granville, the Liberal National MP for Eye in Suffolk, who had served as a captain in the Royal Artillery in 1939–40, suggested that this might have something to do with the fact that stories of heroism during the sinking of the *Lancastria* were known on Merseyside within two or three days of the sinking. It was afterwards given out on German radio but five weeks had elapsed before the BBC referred to the story. There was, said Mr Granville, considerable anxiety in the public mind about the delay:

'In view of the statement of the Prime Minister that he would reveal the losses of warships and merchantmen as soon as possible, does not the Right Honourable Gentleman think that it is better for a statement to be made in this country, rather than that it should come from Germany and America?'

Cooper replied that there were many stories of heroism connected with the Dunkirk evacuation, and this was one that he regretted did not receive the full publicity it deserved. Davie Logan, the Labour MP for Liverpool Scotland, asked why those most concerned were not informed sooner of the ship's loss:

'As one who knew many of the crew who were lost on board that ship, may I ask how it was that the parents were not notified? And why, when it was public property all over the city of Liverpool when the loss occurred, publicity was not given to the people particularly concerned whose sons had gone down to the sea in ships?'

Cooper said that the relatives of those lost were informed as soon as identity was established.

News of the sinking of the *Lancastria* had originally been covered by a D-Notice (Defence Notice). After Dunkirk, Churchill did not want the public to be further demoralised. The D-Notice system that had been introduced in 1912 was in theory only advisory, not legally enforceable, thus newspapers did not have to abide by them. That was true up to a point. Newspapers were issued with guidance and invited to submit stories that might be covered by a D-Notice such as that which applied to the *Lancastria*. The censor would scrutinise these stories and redact them according to the guidelines. Information such as troop movements and weather reports were removed. Anyone publishing a story that was not returned bearing a rubber-stamped 'Passed for Censorship' was liable for prosecution if it were found to contravene the guidelines. In 1940, the still fledgling Ministry of Information, formed on 4 September 1939, was responsible for publicity and propaganda. It had soon run into trouble when it attempted to retrospectively censor news of the British Expeditionary Force's arrival in France. Thereafter it was never going to be a huge success and was at times described by a suspicious Press as 'shambolic and disorganised' even though Press censorship now worked on a principle of self-enforcement. In the meantime, Churchill's well-meaning attempt to cover up – or at least delay for as long as possible – the sinking of the *Lancastria* had annoyed some, while others had found it agonising. For weeks and months afterwards, newspapers carried reports of relatives who did not know what had happened to their loved ones who had perished. Of course, D-Notice or no D-Notice, there could never be an answer to that. Meanwhile, the British just had to trust what they were reading in the newspapers as best they could.

Three months after the sinking of the *Lancastria*, those newspapers were reporting another 'sea barbarity … Nazi mass murder … Hitler's worst crime of the war …' By the start of 1940, with no bombing of major towns and cities, almost 60 per cent of evacuees had returned home, but after Dunkirk, between 13 and 18 June alone, more than 100,000 children were evacuated; in some cases re-evacuated. When the Blitz began on 7 September still more children were sent to what were considered safer areas, not only within Britain but also to other parts of the British Empire, many to stay with relatives or foster parents. Between June and September 1940, through the Children's Overseas Reception Board (CORB) 1,532 children were evacuated to Canada, 577 to Australia, 353 to South Africa and 202 to New Zealand. Some were evacuated to the United States. On 29 August, the SS *Volendam* set sail from Liverpool with 320 children on their way to Halifax, Nova Scotia, and to New York.

The following day the convoy that also included RMS *Rangitata* carrying 113 children bound for New Zealand was attacked by a U-boat. Although the *Volendam* was not sunk she was damaged and her passengers and crew taken off by other ships in the convoy. The only fatality was the ship's purser, who drowned. The 320 children were landed at Greenock and all but two were returned to their families. A delayed-action bomb threatened the Kent home of 10-year-old Michael Brooker, while other circumstances prevented 12-year-old Patricia Allen from returning to her Liverpool home. The two children were given priority status and places on the next available passage. Patricia Allen told a *Liverpool Echo* reporter that she was unperturbed by her experience and that her one desire was to get to Canada and start a new life with friends.

On 17 September 1940, the SS *City of Benares*, a British passenger ship on its way to Canada from Liverpool, carrying ninety evacuated children, was torpedoed by a U-boat in the North Atlantic. Of the 406 people on board, 258 were killed including 81 children. On 23 September a list of those who had perished was published. Patricia Allen and Michael Brooker were among them. The CORB scheme was promptly cancelled.

Chapter Eleven

Look, Duck – and Vanish

'These officers and men … have the strongest desire to attack and come to close quarters with the enemy, wherever he may appear.'

Winston Churchill

On 1 September 1940, the *Sunday Pictorial* launched a new series. The first instalment of 'Home Guard Parade!' explained:

'In this country more than a million of you are standing-to, day and night, Britain's second line of defence, on guard. Some of you are youths; some of you are old. Some of you have, for one reason or another, not been able to join the Services. But you are there, on the village green, outside the thundering workshops, in the city streets, and on the lonely cliff tops, playing your part in the Battle of Britain, on duty in your own service – the Home Guards.'

On Tuesday, 14 May, the Minister of War, Anthony Eden, had made a BBC radio broadcast in which he referred to 'the form of warfare which the Germans have been employing so extensively against Holland and Belgium, namely the dropping of troops by parachute behind the main defensive line'. Eden continued:

'Since the war began, the government has received countless inquiries from all over the kingdom from men of all ages who are, for one reason or another, not at present engaged in military service, and who wish to do something for the defence of their country. Well, now is your opportunity. We want large numbers of such men in Great Britain, who are British subjects, between the ages of 17 and 65, to come forward now and offer their service in order to make assurance doubly sure. The name of the new force, which is now to be raised, will be the Local Defence Volunteers [LDV].'

The following day the *Nottingham Evening Post* reported:

'Men all over Nottinghamshire who, in peace time, trained their guns on rabbits and game, rushed to police stations to enrol last night, immediately after the wireless call for recruits for the Local Defence Volunteers. The LDV are a new section of the Home Front Army. Another name for them might be "The parachutist snipers", for the job of these men, aged between 17 and 65, will be to account for any German parachutist troops who attempt to land in this country. As soon as the announcement was made, many men flung on their hats and coats, and presented themselves to the Nottingham Guildhall. The same thing happened in the suburbs and the country districts. Today, enrolment went on rapidly.'

The *North-Eastern Daily Gazette* told a similar story:

'Throughout Cleveland the response to the call for men for the Local Defence Volunteers has been very encouraging. Men of all trades, professions and ages have poured into police stations in the area and continue to report in large numbers today … at Redcar, Guisborough, Loftus, and in every village and hamlet in Cleveland, the same story was told today of men rushing to join the Local Defence Volunteers, eager to be "off the mark" and delighted at the chance of being able to help their country win the war.'

This was the picture throughout much of the country. In Manchester, the response was 'magnificent, almost overwhelming'. In Birmingham, the rush at times was almost too much for officials. Within hours, hundreds of men in Liverpool had filled in application forms. In Sheffield, men were volunteering by telephone even before Eden had finished his broadcast and within half an hour of his appeal there were long queues at signing-on points in the city. In London men eager to join the LDV besieged every police station.

At Banstead, in Surrey, a beleaguered police inspector said, 'We can't cope with them. We've run out of forms and are carrying on by typing out as many as we can, and telling the rest to come back tomorrow.' In Oxford, university professors and undergraduates rubbed shoulders as they queued patiently. At Chichester, several clergymen were among those who enrolled.

Derby's men were quick to come forward. On the first day, 450 volunteered; at the end of the first week, that number had climbed to more than 1,000. One of the first to enlist in the new force was Alec McWilliams, who went on to become a director of Rolls-Royce. He became a lieutenant in the R-R unit and recalled:

'At first we were equipped with LDV armbands, and later with denim boiler suits. We had to find our own weapons and, in the early stages, these ranged from rifles and pistols to pitchforks and pikestaffs. Our first role was as an anti-sabotage unit. When the sirens sounded and the factory was deserted, the authorities felt that we were open to someone either planting a bomb, or doing some crude sabotage like placing a spoke in one of the machines. As time wore on, we were renamed the Home Guard and were given proper uniforms and weapons, like rifles and Thompson sub-machine guns. Looking back, people were more objective during the war and there wasn't time to indulge in petty differences.'

Lew Patrick reported to his Home Guard unit at Kingsway Drill Hall in Derby after working twelve-hour shifts at the town's Carriage and Wagon Works. He recalled:

'In those days, you never counted the hours or watched the clock. If a job needed doing, you just got on with it. It was nothing to spend twelve hours in a factory and then report for Home Guard duty. Then a few hours' sleep and back to work.'

The government had expected 150,000 men to volunteer for the LDV. Within the first month, 750,000 men had stepped forward and by the end of June the total number of volunteers had risen to over one million, In

July, Eden told the House of Commons that as the response now exceeded 1,300,000 men, it had been decided to temporarily suspend recruiting in the near future, except in districts where the strength had not met immediate requirements. This would enable the provision of equipment for all accepted volunteers to be pressed forward. In the meantime, applicants could continue to register at police stations and would be put in a waiting list.

As Eden had hinted, the story was not the same absolutely everywhere. A few days later, the *Newcastle Chronicle* reported:

'Newcastle still urgently requires hundreds of recruits for the Home Guard. This needs stressing as there is some misapprehension following the statement by Mr Anthony Eden that is has been decided to suspend recruiting in the near future, except in districts where the strength had not met immediate requirements. Newcastle is one of these districts. All men qualified to join the Home Guard should enrol at the nearest police station … so as to take the place of men who leave for the Regular Forces or other reasons.'

Only three days earlier, the same newspaper had told its readers of the more heartening picture nationwide:

'The story of the rapid growth of the Home Guard is an amazing one. Men who have fought in the last war have jumped to the call so that over a million have now enrolled. This force has given the old sweats an opportunity of doing their bit for their country … One volunteer I know, who fought in the Great War and was wounded, said, when handed a rifle: "This is like old times," for he carried a weapon many miles in Flanders in 1915. And fired it, too!'

Wherever they joined, men were ignoring the fact that they were expected to fight highly trained, well-armed German troops using nothing but shotguns, air rifles, old hunting rifles, museum pieces, bayonets, knives and pieces of gas pipe with knives or bayonets welded on the end. Eventually, more conventional arms would be issued, albeit mainly of First World War vintage or else of American or Canadian manufacture, and better training would transform the original rag-tag army – unkindly known in some quarters as 'Look, Duck and Vanish' – into an organisation that may well have proved an inconvenience to German paratroopers.

On 23 July 1940, Eden announced in the House of Commons that an Order of Council would be made, changing the name. The new force would henceforth be known as the Home Guard. What would become a legend in British history was born. The London correspondent of the *Liverpool Post* was not entirely convinced:

> 'The Prime Minister's example in referring to the Local Defence Volunteers as the Home Guard is now to be followed in all but official references to that body. There would be difficulties about making a formal change, not the least of which would be the costly one of changing armlets. In any case, the initials fit more easily on to an armlet than the longer word would.'

In fact, Eden had already announced that new armlets would be issued with the initials 'HG'.

It also meant that area commanders who had just been authorised to carry a blue-bordered pennant in their cars, with the letters 'LDV' would now have to scrap these for the new version. Eventually, all Home Guard would be issued with uniforms modelled on those of regular soldiers. Priorities would go first to platoons around the coast until sufficient had been produced to supply every member. For the moment, though, an armlet and a bread knife tied to a broom handle was the order of the day.

The original idea – that this citizens' army would try to delay invading German forces until the Regular Army could be rushed to the scene – was a response to what was already happening up and down the country. As an invasion became more likely, there were reports of bands of civilians arming themselves with shotguns, air rifles and pitchforks, ready to face the Hun. The government had two options; to quash these grass-roots resistance fighters or to harness them into an official organisation. The Local Defence Volunteers were formed without any budget or any staff. Even as what became the Home Guard developed into something resembling a military force, its relationship with the War Office was generally an uneasy one. Lieutenant-General Sir Henry

Royds Pownall, the LDV's first inspector general, complained, 'They are a troublesome and querulous lot ... there is mighty little pleasing them, and the minority is always noisy.' In the interests of balance, it should be noted that historian Brian D. Osborne, in his account of the Home Guard in Scotland, wrote that while Lieutenant-General Pownall – who was chief of general staff for the British Expeditionary Force in France and Belgium until the fall of France in May 1940 – might have appeared 'a high quality appointment', in fact Field Marshal Montgomery thought him 'completely useless'.

There was no shortage of opinion. Writing in the *Aberdeen Press and Journal* on 22 July 1940, 'Military Man' highlighted teething problems, although noting that the LDV was only two months old and that there were bound to be things going wrong at first 'through misunderstanding, over-zealousness and so forth'. He quoted a correspondent who had told him:

'Many local section leaders of the LDV seem still to concentrate too much on platoon drill and other parade exercises rather than on training us to use our initiative. I have in mind several sections of a large town where, although LDVs have been in existence a month, training has been confined to forming fours, half-right turns etc. In one case a night patrol did not take place because the section leader spent nearly two hours arguing on the best method to perform a right about-turn.'

'Military Man' commented:

'If Hitler comes next week it will not make much difference whether that section understands right-about turns or not ... the basic idea of all drills is to ensure that a man will do the right thing as a matter of habit when the bombs are falling or the shells are bursting. I have heard of odd cases of men who, when asked to take a patrol on a certain day, are inclined to answer: "Well, I may be able to do it but that depends on other engagements." That is wrong. If you join you must be prepared to sacrifice other engagements except in cases of extreme emergency. A good many problems must be settled

in a friendly spirit on the spot … A reader, for instance, tells me of
a case where the use of the Territorials drill hall and its miniature
rifle range have been refused to the LDVs. This seems absurd …'

He also felt that the Local Defence Volunteers would continue to be known
by that title, 'despite the premier's use of the term "Home Guards".'

Teething problems there certainly were, especially when it came to
encouraging the use of initiative. In the Commons on 16 July, Eden said
that in some cases private individuals had erected defence works without
consulting military authorities and that many had been dismantled
because they were ill-sited. 'The military should be consulted before
works are undertaken.'

Arthur Woodburn, the Scottish Labour MP who had been imprisoned
as a conscientious objector during the First World War, remarked that if
1,000 German cyclists were riding over the country, then the LDV would
not have time to consult the military authorities. Eden replied, 'I do not
share his apprehension of 1,000 German cyclists – or of a much smaller
number.'

The duty was taken seriously. In July, Edward Grant, a junior master
blacksmith, appeared before Banff Sheriff Court accused of threatening an
employee with dismissal while he was on duty as a Home Guard. Grant had
originally driven George Low, an apprentice blacksmith in his employment,
to his Home Guard post but later returned and told Low that if he did not
accompany him back to work, he would be given his cards. The Home
Guard commander reported Grant to the police and he was arrested.
Grant's defence was that he was busy with work of national importance
and when he learned that three other Home Guards – two assistant grocers
and a gardener-chauffeur – had not been called on for duty, he committed
the offence out of a sense of frustration and exasperation. Grant was told
that his was a grave offence, seeking to put private convenience and interest
before the service of his country. He was fined £5.

The new force soon caught the public's imagination. In September,
the Reverend R.D. Jones, writing in the *Western Mail*, said:

'Two young Home Guards were sent to patrol a stretch of railway
line. As one of them tramped along his beat he got his foot wedged

in the points and fell headlong. His companion, hearing the crash, ran to his assistance. But it was pitch dark. He caught his foot in the signalling wires, and went sprawling, driving his bayonet deep into the ground in the process. I have nothing, however, but admiration for these men, who, after a full day's work, are willing to spend wakeful nights on our roads or our bleak and lonely hillsides, watching for the first sign of enemy action.'

Churchill told the nation:

'… Behind the Regular Army we have more than one million of the Local Defence Volunteers, or, as they are much better called, the Home Guard. These officers and men, a large proportion of whom have been through the last war, have the strongest desire to attack and come to close quarters with the enemy, wherever he may appear. Should the invader come to Britain there will be no placid lying down of the people before him, as we have seen, alas, in other countries. We shall defend every village, every town, every city. The vast majority of London itself, fought street by street, could easily devour an entire hostile army, and we would rather see London laid in ashes and ruins than that it should be tamely and abjectly enslaved.'

German radio was naturally unimpressed, and turned to sarcasm:

'Mr Churchill said things might break loose, perhaps tonight, perhaps next week, perhaps never. We wonder if Mr Churchill was counting the buttons in his waistcoat when he said that. The answer is, not this week, neither next, and certainly not never, but very definitely sometime.'

Commenting on the figures given of Home Guard men under arm, the German broadcast continued, 'Under what arms? Broomsticks, or the arms of the local public house, with pots of beer and darts in their hands?' As for Churchill's promise that he would rather see London lying in ruin than capitulate, 'He would deny the British public the blessing and calm which had descended on Paris.'

A week later the German mood had changed. An English-language broadcast from Bremen howled that the Home Guard was:

'a contravention of international law ... Although the British people are misled, they are nevertheless murderers, but the vilest criminals of all are the British government, who started such illegal activities. The British would do well to heed the German warning.'

The Italian newspaper *Popolo di Roma* agreed:

'England seems to regard the Churchill war as a mass attack by civilians. The formation of such crops of hedgehoppers is contrary to international convention. Such a violation of international law justifies the adoption of suitable measures. The result of such illegal British measures will lead to a frightful war of destruction, the responsibility of which will rest with the British government alone.'

At home there was no shortage of opinion on how the Home Guard should best be used. Some of the advice came from controversial sources. Major-General John Frederick Charles 'Boney' Fuller was a retired senior British Army officer, a military historian and an author. He also supported the organised fascist movement – after retiring from the Army in 1933, he sat on the Policy Directorate of Sir Oswald Mosley's British Union of Fascists, and in the 1961 edition of his book *The Reformation of War* he would announce that the wrong side had won the Second World War, denouncing Churchill and Roosevelt as being too stupid to see that Hitler could have been the saviour of the West against the Soviet Union.

In July 1940, as one of a series of syndicated articles that he wrote for British newspapers, Fuller touched on the 'Battle Role of Home Guard'. After roundly condemning the wall of concrete that was Maginot Line – in his words 'The Tombstone of France' – in that the prophets who said that the French could safely crouch behind it until the Germans had committed suicide by attacking it were 'hideously wrong', Fuller held that the art of successful warfare through history could be expressed in three words; Guard, Move, Hit. He had a clearly defined view of what the Home Guard's role should be:

'We have 1,500,00 soldiers in this country; we have 1,000,000 Home Guards, and so long as our feed holds out and our ships hold the seas, we have nothing to fear from a direct invasion. That is to say, if we modify our rat and rabbit tactics and organise these 2,500,000 stout-hearted men as the Maginot Line should have been – namely on the idea of mobility. To meet and frustrate invasion, we want two things: bastions and sally parties ... a reasoned combination between shield and sword ... between semi-static defence and fully mobile offence, the first being provided by the Home Guard, and the second by the Army.

'Remember this: the Home Guard, however stout-hearted he may be, he is not a disciplined soldier, and since discipline is an essential of mobile warfare, therefore his role is to guard and move ... there must be a definite tactical separation between the duties of the Home Guard and the soldier. The first should fight defensively ... the first should be provided with entrenchments on our shorelines and, behind them, step by step inland. He fights, and when he retires it is from defensive works; his mobility consists in moving back slowly, always protected by a shield, whilst the soldier should move like lightning and strike like a thunderbolt. Have I made myself clear? GUARD, MOVE, HIT: foot-play backwards for the Home Guards; foot-play forwards for the soldier.'

Fuller was not the only man with extreme views to involve himself in how the Home Guard should operate. In July 1940, Tom Wintringham, who had commanded the British Battalion of the International Brigade during the Spanish Civil War, opened an unofficial training camp for Home Guards at Osterley Park in North London, where he taught street fighting and guerrilla warfare. Wintringham also wrote articles in the *Daily Mirror* and *Picture Post*, in which he championed the Home Guard but with the motto 'A people's war for a people's peace.' In October 1940, the Regular Army took charge of Home Guard training at Osterley Park. The following April, Wintringham resigned. Despite his support for the Home Guard he was never allowed to join an organisation that barred anyone with Communist or Fascist backgrounds.

In October, as the days drew shorter – and no invasion had yet happened – the *Manchester Evening News* wondered what would happen to the Home Guard 'in certain cities during the winter':

'Unless an attempted invasion takes place, there is a grave danger that its strength in many areas will gradually fall away. The members of the Home Guard, the majority of them hard workers during the day, have given up their leisure time and much-needed sleep at nights to meet emergency. There is a danger that many may feel, as the emergency appears less, that it is not worthwhile continuing. To meet this attitude of mind, the best method is to reduce their duties to the utmost and increase their training in weapons other than the rifle. By this means the strain will be relieved, their interest maintained, and their potential usefulness increased. There is no reason at present why police and military should not carry out all the tasks which are properly theirs but which have been given over to the Home Guard during the summer months.'

In fact, this proposed guerrilla army was already finding a new role. As they waited for an invasion to begin, the Home Guard acted as additional eyes and ears for regular troops. They knew their area well and so could identify strangers. They asked to see identity cards, handing over to the police anybody who could not produce one. At a time when there was a heightened fear of Fifth Columnists in the midst of the general public, the local knowledge of the Home Guard was considered vital. They were also responsible for removing road signs and any other clues that might prove helpful to an invader.

The Scotsman, meanwhile, reported that one of its staff, who had taken part in a Home Guard exercise, complained about the reluctance of some members of the organisation to consider themselves 'dead':

'Having directed a withering fire in the direction of several HG's attacking his post, our colleague was astonished to see them acting as though they were still very much alive. It needed some expostulation on his part to convince them that they were already shot to pieces, and, consequently, very much dead.

'To lay down one's life in mimic warfare does not call for very great sacrifice. The position of a corpse in military manoeuvres is not, by and large, an unsatisfactory one. Theoretically dead, he may, if he so wishes, indulge in pleasant occupations normally reserved for the living. He may relax at his ease, his mind undisturbed by tactical worries. He may, if he chooses, retire behind a bush and consume ice-cream. He may, if he interprets his role literally, insist on being carried home in solemn comfort.

'Yet surprisingly few mock warriors show themselves willing to embrace death on the field. They find it easy to assure themselves that they bear charmed lives, and that bullets automatically deflect before reaching them. With supreme disregard for personal safety, they expose themselves to furious fire, and laugh at death. The truth is that there may be something rather humiliating about dying on manoeuvres, Even though one may have, relatively speaking, met a hero's death, it seems very unheroic to lie snugly in the mud watching with sluggish indolence, one's comrades–in–arms smashing their way through to glory.'

Occasionally, Home Guards made headlines for the wrong reason. In October 1940, hammer driver Christopher Robinson (25) was found guilty of stealing sugar, cocoa, polish and other items to the value of 13s 10d from Coventry Co-operative Society while he was on duty by a bomb crater. Despite being told that Robinson had displayed great courage in attempting to rescue people from a wrecked house, the magistrate said, 'You are a disgrace to the Home Guard.' Two months later, an 18-year-old Home Guard called Francis John Southall, of Coventry, was sentenced to one month's hard labour after stealing from a bombed shop in the city. One of the items he took was a chest expander. In his defence, his stepfather told the court that Southall wanted to get fit so that he could join the Regular Army. The youth said, 'I didn't realise I was stealing.' A headline in a local newspaper put it rather more strongly. 'Home Guard Sentenced For Looting.'

The same month, a 45-year-old Home Guard was sentenced to 12 months' hard labour after stealing two 1lb-tins of boiled sweets, worth 2s 8d from a shop that had just been damaged during an air-raid on

Southall. William Banker, whose Home Guard unit was attached to the London Transport Passenger Board, had been detained by another Home Guard. In September, 41-year-old John Henry Louis Gichero of Stockport, was fined £5 for driving a car while under the influence of drink. The court was told that he was a member of Home Guard mobile unit. Home Guard William Farrington (46) was fined £1 for assaulting an air-raid warden who accused him of showing an unscreened light. Leigh magistrates dismissed the lighting charge but took a dim view of a Home Guard having a midnight tussle with an ARP warden.

There were also tragic accidents. In September, in Wolverhampton, a 16-year-old partially deaf boy, Alan Chadwick, was shot and killed by the Home Guard while riding his bicycle. He did not stop when challenged. In Holloway, London, an 18-year-old Home Guard, Henry Driver, was accidentally shot through the head by a colleague who did not realise that his rifle was loaded. St Pancras coroner W. Bentley Purchase said, 'Steps should be taken to impress on the people concerned that this sort of thing should not happen again.'

'I can assure you that steps have been taken,' replied the company commander, Charles Hambourg.

Keeping loaded firearms on domestic premises was always likely to produce a tragedy. In October, 38-year-old Ethel Louisa Perry died instantly at her Merseyside bungalow when the rifle that her Home Guard husband was cleaning was accidentally fired. 'The couple had been married for a number of years and were described as a very devoted pair,' reported the *Liverpool Evening Express*.

On 10 August, 19-year-old Ronald Nisbet became the first member of the Home Guard to be killed in action. Nisbet, a member of the railway section of the 23rd Durham Battalion, was on patrol with two colleagues during an air-raid on South Shields. The anti-aircraft barrage was so intense that the men decided to return to their shelter. As they entered, Nisbet was hit on the head by a piece of shrapnel and died in hospital. His end was a tragedy made even more so by the fact that it was his sense of duty that led to it. After missing the previous night's patrol through illness, he had turned out on a night when he would normally have been at home when the raid took place. Ronald Nisbet was the first of many. Over the course of the war, aside from deaths in accidents, 1,206 Home

Guards were killed on duty during air attacks, or later died of their wounds.

As the threat of imminent invasion receded but the Blitz intensified, on 10 November, Sir Edward Grigg, Joint Under-Secretary of State for War, told the Commons:

'The Home Guard is the product of two forces. One of them is the force of events, and the other, which usually rises superior to the force of events, is the force of British character and tradition. When the world was darkened by the eclipse of France, one fact stood out. That was the extent to which mechanised raiding parties had terrorised whole countryside, destroying communications and dislocating the national life. The result in a matter of days was universal confusion, crippling both the will and the power to resist. The horror of that spectacle stirred this country to its depths. At that time men of all ages in all parts of the country were eating their hearts out because for one reason or another they had no opportunity of offering military service of one kind or another. Some were too old; others were debarred by their occupations from joining the Fighting Services. Therefore, the demand for some opportunity of service was intense. From end to end the countrymen swore that what had happened in France should not happen here. That was the origin of the Home Guard. My Right Honourable Friend [Anthony Eden] realised both the greatness of the need and the strength, indeed the intensity, of the demand. He made his appeal only six months ago, on 14 May, and the Home Guard is the result. I am sure the House will agree that it is a lusty infant for six months, strong of constitution, powerful of lung and avid, like all healthy infants, for supplies.'

The MP for Fulham West, Dr Edith Summerskill, chipped in, 'It is of only one sex.'

Sir Edward replied, 'Most are infants, I believe.' Not quite infants, but not Dad's Army either. By the time the Home Guard was stood down in late 1944, half of the four million who had served were under 27 and a third were under 18.

Sir Edward said:

> 'I have seen it suggested that the Regular Army leaders adopted
> a step-motherly attitude to the Home Guard. Really, nothing is
> further from the fact. The Regular Army leaders appreciated the
> military value of this Force from the very start and, despite the
> heavy administrative burden, which the commands are carrying,
> they did everything to promote its efficiency and prosper its growth.
> Co-operation between the Regular Army and the Home Guard
> practically everywhere has been excellent; indeed, the organisation
> and training of the Home Guard are least advanced where it has had
> least opportunity of contact with Regular troops.'

He told the House:

> 'It is Britain incarnate, an epitome of British character in its gift for
> comradeship in trouble, its resourcefulness at need, its deep love of
> its own land, and its surging anger at the thought that any invader
> should set foot on our soil. That is the make-up of the Home Guard.
> St George, St Andrew, St David – yes, and St Crispin – are alive
> and marching in its democratic ranks.'

Dr Summerskill wanted to know, 'What about Boadicea?'

The Home Guard certainly provided some amusement. On 19 August
1940, the *Daily Mirror* told the story of a Home Guard unit that brought
down a dive-bomber with rifle fire, then hurried home to tell their wives
all about it, only to be greeted with complaints that they were an hour late
for Sunday lunch. 'Why do these Germans have to come at dinner time?'
the wife of Captain H.S. Prince wanted to know. 'Most inconsiderate.
They've spoiled your meal.' 'I'm afraid our boiled beef and dumplings
came first with the wife – but I wouldn't have missed the scrap,' Captain
Prince told the newspaper.

George Watson, who was later promoted to wing commander and
awarded the DFC after locating the German battleship Tirpitz at anchor
in a Norwegian fjord, said:

'In 1940 I was flying a Miles Magister over Allestree Park in Derby. Our brief was to give the Home Guard a chance to guess at what height we were flying and let them have a bit of aiming practice as well. Only when we got back to base did we realise they were using live ammunition. One bullet had gone straight between my knees. The young officer is charge told an inquiry: "We thought they were armour-plated. In any case, we never thought we'd hit them!"'

As we have seen earlier, initiative was not always rewarded. 1978, J.M. Seward of Seaton in Devon recalled:

'In 1940 I joined what was still the Local Defence Volunteers in Cheltenham. My occupation as a plumber and slater, plus my age group – I was then 31 – put me in the deferred call-up class for military service. I owned a motorcycle so I became the despatch rider. I was also very keen to improve on anything that I considered to be out-of-date thinking.

'One sunny Sunday morning, seventy-two of us went to the local shooting butts to fire six rounds each at targets 2,500 yards away. We arrived about 9.30am and left about 7pm. But about 60 per cent of that time was taken up using flags to signal back target hits. Now I'd been building radios since I was 11, so when we returned to the range three weeks later, I produced a simple device with a "speak/listen" switch together with loudspeakers. It was a great success and reduced by more than half the time we spent on the range. We were getting the "target hit" signal straight away rather than waiting for the flags. The only thing was that it cost £4.10s, which I had to pay.

'We also had to guard a length of railway line from nightfall to daybreak, with instructions that if a German paratrooper dropped in, we had to disarm him, tie his hands behind his back and walk him to HQ, leaving some of our men to stay on guard. It seemed to me that we needed to inform HQ immediately, but that drum beating was a little "old hat" while smoke signals would work only in daytime. So I constructed another radio transmitter, one that could have us reporting any incident to HQ within seconds.

'I combed numerous radio shops and second-hand dealers, and put an advertisement in the local newspaper, and eventually I had sufficient parts to build my radio. Five weeks later I had all I needed, including an alarm clock for transmitting a "tick-tock" to test it. It worked like a dream and so I decided to show it to our local MP, Daniel Lipson. I took only the receiver to his house and assured him that we wouldn't be breaking the law, as there was nothing illegal about receiving radio signals, only sending them. When he heard the "tick-tock" being transmitted from my home, he was taken aback and told me to put the whole thing out of sight and that he'd contact me in due course. Well, when his answer came it was: "No can do".

'I knew what would happen next, so I put the apparatus away, together with a postcard that read: "Made by J.M.S. for use by HG – Maybe. Date completed and checked 1 October 1940. Cost of construction (pair) £14.10s 0d." Then I waited. Seventy-two hours later there was a knock on our front door. There stood two detectives. They had it on good authority that I had in my possession instruments for the transmission of radio signals contrary to Section 8 of the Defence of the Realm Act. I was taken to the police station where my story was taken down and I was put in a cell, together with a deserter who was waiting for the Military Police. I thought: "Isn't it marvellous? He's in here for shirking his duty and I'm in here for overdoing mine."

'Finally, in the early evening, they took me back upstairs. Some technical bods had examined my radio and I was free to go. It was smiles all round. They even laid on a car. My first stop was home to pick up my Home Guard kit. My second stop was the Home Guard HQ, where I handed in my resignation. I was fed-up of playing at soldiers. The following day, my old CO asked me if I'd go with him to see the officer commanding the Home Guard in the area. The OC thanked me for my efforts in trying to improve communications and make my unit one of the most up-to-date. He said that my radio was being sent to Southern Command for testing, but later I was told that it had been impounded "for the duration of the war".

'Just after that Christmas I received my call-up papers. I passed my medical and then was interviewed by a selection officer. I noticed that my card had one difference to everyone else's: there was a dotted red line under my name. I wondered if it was some sort of code, some hint about my tangle with the authorities over my radio apparatus. Anyway, the selection officer said that he thought it unlikely that I would be called up – and I never was. I still think I was right, though, in doing what I did.'

Harold Richardson of Derby recalled his days as a Home Guard:

'In 1940 I was 18, and my pal, Arthur, 17. Only those who experienced those nervous days, after the fall of France, can appreciate the fervour of patriotism that gripped the country and caused Arthur and myself among a million others, young and not so young, to sign up for what was then called the Local Defence Volunteers.

'To begin with, we were put through the complications of arms drill by "old sweats", who showed much restraint each time rifles evaded stiff fingers and clattered to the ground. One of the ways to stop a tank, we were told, was to place an upturned dinner plate on the road. The tank driver, mistaking this for an anti-tank mine, would probably bring his tank to a halt. The rest was easy: wait for the tank hatch to open then lob in a grenade. It sounded all right and the younger ones especially seemed to be taking it in. But I had a little nagging doubt myself. If this neat trick has already been tried out in France, then it couldn't have worked all that well.

'Anyway, after a fortifying drink or two had helped us ready ourselves to take on the whole Nazi army if necessary, Arthur and me set off around 9.30 on a Friday evening to report for our first night guard duty. Searching for our headquarters, a deserted farmhouse, we had just crossed a boggy field when all at once a voice came from out of the darkness.

'First of all it said: "Stop!" Then: "Halt! I mean. Halt! Who goes there?"

'Arthur said: "Us." There was a bit of a pause. "You can't say that," went the voice, sort of indignant. "You gotta say it. You gotta say friend or foe."

'Arthur obliged: "Friend or foe."

'After a longer pause, I could just make out this shadowy figure approaching us, holding what looked like a broom handle with a bayonet tied to it. "You gotta be one thing or the other," it complained, getting nearer. "I mean, I'm supposed to make you say it." By then the sharp end of the bayonet was waving close to our faces. "You gotta say it."

'Before Arthur could further complicate our arrival, I answered: "We're LDV."

'At the broomstick end of the weapon, the shadow took on a tin-hatted, white disc of a face wearing glasses. "How do I know you're not just saying that? For all I know you could be foe."

'Thanks to the beer, Arthur was now getting a tad aggressive: "We ain't got bloody parachutes on. We got armbands on, see! Ain't you got no torch?"

'The bayonet lowered itself. "We're still waiting for new batteries, like. Hold on though, I've got some matches here. I'd better make sure, hadn't I?"

'After some scraping, a flaring match broke through the blackout while this fearless guard scrutinised our armbands. We could then see he was a long-faced youth with two prominent teeth. "Yeah, that's right, you got armbands on," he conceded. "Bit late, ain't you?"

'Arthur was now totally fed up: "We'll be a bloody sight later before you've done."

'What a pantomime!'

A pantomime maybe, but they were ever-ready. On 25 July 1940, George Hicks, the Labour MP for Woolwich East, made a wireless broadcast on the BBC, in which he described a Home Guard training:

'They were raw, they were awkward, some were elderly, and some – like myself – showed signs of living a too sedentary life. But they were willing, eager and full of fighting spirit. Many were veterans of the last war, Seeing them, and knowing their thoroughness and indomitable courage, I thought of the warm welcome the enemy would get, should invasion be attempted. Britain bristles these days, It is armed and alert ...'

Chapter Twelve

Frightened and Exiled

'I am afraid that the authorities have been somewhat stampeded against their better judgement.'

Major Victor Cazalet MP

In August 1940, a sad little procession, each person carrying a suitcase, made its way across a busy road to the Midland railway station in Derby. One hundred German and Austrian women, some of them nuns, had been arrested and were on the first stage of their journey to an internment camp on the Isle of Man. The scene was being repeated throughout the country. Since the outbreak of the First World War, all aliens over the age of 16 had been required to register their details at local police offices. When Britain again found herself at war with Germany, some 73,000 German and Austrian citizens resident in the UK found themselves immediately classed as enemy aliens. Faced with a similar situation to that of August 1914, the government acted quickly. By 28 September 1939, the Aliens Department of the Home Office had set up some 120 internment tribunals across the UK, where government officials and local magistrates examined the credentials of every registered alien over 16, many of whom were represented by a member of the German Jewish Aid Committee. The tribunals divided the aliens into three categories: Category A were to be interned; Category B would to be exempt from internment but subject to the restrictions decreed by Special Order; Category C would be exempt from both internment and restrictions. Just under 600 'high-risk' aliens were interned immediately and by February 1940, the tribunals' work on vetting the remainder was almost complete. A large majority of aliens, around 65,000, were classed as Category C, although, surprisingly, 6,500 Jews who had fled to the UK before the war to escape Nazi persecution were classified Category B, and 569 Jews were placed in Category A, which meant that they would be transferred under guard to internment camps. There were various camps on the Isle of Man – at Hutchinson, Metropole, Mooragh, Onchan and Port Erin – and others in and around London, Manchester, Liverpool, Birmingham, Bury, Huyton, Seaton, Paignton, and at Lingfield and Kempton Park racecourses. From June 1940, the Warth Mills camp near Bury received thousands of internees, many of them destined for deportation to Canada.

By May 1940, with the war having taken a dramatic turn and the risk of invasion high, a further 8,000 Germans and Austrians resident in Britain found themselves interned irrespective of their category. When Italy declared war on Britain on 10 June, it was the turn of resident Italians to face the tribunals, and some 4,000 known to be members of Benito Mussolini's *Partito Nazionale Fascista* (PNF) were interned along with all Italians between the ages of 16 and 70 who, though displaying no outward support of Il Duce, had lived in the UK for fewer than twenty years. At the outbreak of the war there had been 19,000 Italians living in Britain, many of them in Scotland, most of them having lived there for decades.

The increase in the number of internees in 1940 was now providing a major headache for the government. Enemy prisoners-of-war also had to be accommodated. Quite simply, the UK was running out of places to keep thousands of aliens locked up. The governments of Canada and Australia stepped in and between June 24 and 10 July, more than 7,5000 internees were shipped to the Dominions. At 7.58am on 2 July, tragedy struck when the 15,500-ton SS *Arandora Star*, a British passenger ship of the Blue Star Line, was sunk about 125 nautical miles off Malin Head, County Donegal, torpedoed by German submarine U-47 commanded by 32-year-old Gunther Prien. The *Arandora Star* had been en route St John's, Newfoundland. On board were 479 German internees, 734 Italian internees, 86 German prisoners-of-war and 200 military guards. The master, 12 officers, 42 crewmen, 37 guards, 470 Italians and 243 Germans were lost. The survivors were picked up by the Canadian destroyer HMCS *St Laurent* and landed at Greenock.

The British press was quick to condemn the action – albeit in the fog of war slightly exaggerating what was already a tragic loss of life and also using it as propaganda against a 'cowardly' enemy, both on the U-Boat and on the *Arandora Star* herself. The *Daily Herald* headline was stark and to the point. 'U-Boat Sinks Liner, Kills 968 Germans and Italians.' The newspaper quoted one of the survivors, a soldier, '... the Italians made a wild scramble for the lifeboats, pushing everyone aside in their eagerness ... I watched internees trying to sweep soldiers and sailors from the rafts.' Bosun's mate Taff Williams said, 'It was a disgusting sight, a show of cowardice that I have never witnessed before. Women and children would have behaved ever so much more bravely.' 'Nazis And Italians Panic As Ship Goes Down – Refusal To Let Englishmen Climb Into Boats,' screamed the *Gloucestershire Echo*.

The Scotsman commented:

> 'The German Navy has achieved another triumph – it has sent to the bottom of the sea the *Arandora Star* ... carrying 1,500 German prisoners-of-war and Italian internees. About 1,000 persons have been saved and about the same number must have perished ... Even in the midst of this tragedy one must pause for a moment to consider what the German prisoners-of-war and the Italians who have come safely through the ordeal think now of the unrestricted warfare that Germany is waging against peaceful commerce on the sea ... Life is cheap in Nazi reckoning ...'

There were reports that British soldiers had shot at lifeboats to prevent the Italians escaping. The surviving Italians were shipped back to Liverpool from where, the following week, they were at sea again, this time aboard HMT *Dunera*, bound for internment camps in Australia. During the 57-day voyage, the internees were subjected to humiliating treatment and dreadful conditions. Many had their possessions stolen or destroyed by British military guards, some of whom had themselves been released from prison to help the war effort and who were known as 'Soldiers of the King's Pardon' and were serving in the Pioneer Corps, although the guards also included regulars from the Royal Norfolks, Suffolks and the Queen's Own Royal West Kent Regiment. The British government subsequently paid a total of £35,000 in compensation to internees who had been so hideously treated on the *Dunera*.

At home, despite the stories of cowardice among the internees, the fate of the *Arandora Star* began to sway public opinion. Three weeks after

the sinking of the ship laden with internees, the *News Chronicle* carried a
story of seventy-five families from College Buildings, Wentworth Street
in London's East End who had signed a petition for the release of three
local traders who had been interned the previous week. The petition said
that the trio had 'conducted their businesses across the road from the
entrance to College Buildings for between thirty and forty years'. The
paper reported that 'half the inhabitants are Jews and half Christians, but
in the homes of all there is equal indignation and sorrow'.

The wholesale internment of 'enemy aliens' was now being questioned.
That year, Françoise Lafitte, a researcher with Political and Economic
Planning and, later in the war, a journalist with *The Times*, published
his *The Internment of Aliens* in the Penguin Special series. The book
highlighted the governmental panic in the rounding-up of people who
were already refugees from fascism. Lafitte's description of internees'
often appalling living conditions provoked widespread outrage.

In January 1940, an anonymous London journalist, writing a
syndicated article, had painted a rosy picture of one such tribunal, held
at an elementary school, where a police constable stood by the door, there
were no wigs or gowns, and aliens could not employ counsel but a friend
could testify to their good character.

A young German told the presiding magistrate that he had come to
England to be a student but instead took a job as a photographer. The
young man declared that he would like to work or fight for England. The
magistrate told him:

> 'Very well, I will grant you a B certificate. You will not be interned
> but you will not be allowed to own a car, so long as you live in this
> country, nor a camera. And if you go more than 5 miles from where
> you are living you must tell the police first. Do you understand?'

The young men nodded and went out 'relief showing on his thin, drawn
face.'

The next case was a 'young Berlin Jewess, about twenty years of age,
trim and cultured in appearance. She was wearing country clothes'. She
had come to England to work as an artist in an advertising agency but
the war had meant that business was slack and she had been released

and went to work in a garment factory before moving on to a farm in Middlesex. 'I heard many appeals for land workers, and I was anxious to be of real use during the war. I had a little experience on a relative's farm in Germany.' 'All right,' said the magistrate, 'C certificate.'

The reporter continued:

'She goes out smiling … and so the work goes on, sorting out the 50,000 Germans and Austrians in a hundred tribunals up and down the country; picking out the one or two in a hundred who may be dangerous, freeing the scores who mean us well. These frightened, exiled men and women come out with a new respect for the swiftness, fairness and gentleness of British justice.'

Yet in the House of Lords on 6 August 1940, the noted pacifist Lord Faringdon told the stories of men who definitely should not have been on the *Arandora Star*:

'I am not going to inflict a great many cases upon your lordships, but I cannot forebear mentioning two cases of definite anti-Nazis who were on board that ship and who lost their lives. The first was one Karl Olbrisch, who was born in 1902 in Essen. He was a metal worker by profession and a former member of the Reichstag expelled by Hitler on his accession to power. He was arrested by the Gestapo in 1933 and sentenced to three years in the penitentiary and a year in a concentration camp. After his release he went to Czechoslovakia and came to this country in October 1938, on a Czech interim passport. He was maintained in this country by the Czech Refugee Trust Fund until January 1940, when he was interned. The other is Louis Weber, a member of the International Transport Union and formerly of the German Seamen's Union. After Hitler's accession to power he signed on as a sailor in neutral ships. He thought that if he came as an anti-fascist on a neutral ship to England he would be considered as anti-fascist and not be interned. He was, however, interned on arrival and was put into Warner's Camp, Seaton, Devon. He organised in the camp a trade union group, which was directed against the interned Nazis. That case is one of the very usual complaints, which I shall have occasion to repeat: the mélange, or inconsiderate mixing, of Nazis and anti-Nazis in this camp. We understand from another place that something is being done to rectify this state of affairs. But I should like to submit that neither of those men, on their records, ought ever to have been interned at all. Those are absolutely watertight cases in which it seems to me there should not have been any possible doubt of the men's sympathies.'

Faringdon gave further examples of aliens who should not have been interned:

'In addition I would mention one or two similar cases of men who were rescued from the *Arandora Star*, cases which seem to me to be inexplicable and inexcusable. One is that of Kurt Regner, who was born on 4 August 1912, in Baden, near Vienna. He is an Austrian lawyer. This man was one of the most active members in the Socialist Student Movement, and as a lawyer he defended working-class people in trials. He was one of the instigators of the anti-Nazi demonstration on 11 March 1938, in Baden, near Vienna. He was beaten up and had to flee during the night into Czechoslovakia. He was brought over to England by the Hicem group of the Czech Refugee Trust Fund as one of the most endangered refugees. In this country he was secretary of the Austrian Centre Branch in Liverpool. I should not have thought there was much question about that man's antecedents. Then there is Karl Mayerhoefler, born on 21 December 1911, in St Peter Freienstein, Austria. He is an Austrian Socialist who came over to this country on 22 January 1939, as refugee. His fiancée is a Jewess and he wanted to marry her in England. I should have thought that this man's Austrian Socialist background was a fairly good guarantee of his sentiments towards the German invader.

'I would also refer to the cases of Ernst Seemann, a member of the Austrian Socialist Youth Movement, and Michael Glass, searched for by the Gestapo in Vienna. Then there is the case of Valentin Wittke, born in 1904 in Marienburg, Germany, who worked as a cabinetmaker and later as a ships' joiner, one of the leading officials of the workers' organisation. I do not think that I need remind your Lordships that under the Nazi regime no one is in more danger than organisers of labour and trade union movements. This man, as a town councillor, fought for the interests of the anti-fascist workers, and in 1933 organised the collection of money for political prisoners and their relatives. This was betrayed to the Gestapo, and he had to flee to Czechoslovakia. He came to England and was interned by the decision of the tribunal in York – it would be interesting to know on what grounds, in October, 1939 [he was] sent to Seaton camp. His wife was interned at the same time and spent the winter and spring in Holloway prison. She is now in the Isle of Man.'

There was already disquiet in Parliament. In the House of Commons debate on refugees on 10 July 1940, the Conservative MP for Chippenham, Major Victor Cazalet, had referred to the 'wholly un-English attitude' that encouraged mass internment and called upon 'the tradition of this island for many centuries to give a welcome and asylum to all those who were persecuted in other lands'. He told the House that complete disregard had been shown of the merits of individual cases. It was inexcusable, he said, that large numbers of people should have been kept in internment when they ought to have been released. British workers had been turned out of jobs because vital men had been interned. Worst of all, Nazis and Jews had been mixed in the same camp. He said, 'I am afraid that the authorities have been somewhat stampeded against their better judgement.'

In the same debate, two female MPs, Mavis Tate (Conservative, Frome) and Eleanor Rathbone (Independent, Combined English Universities), were in turn loudly cheered by hundreds of their male colleagues as they argued that the government had been too harsh with men and women who had escaped from Nazi terrorism. Rathbone, a fervent campaigner for family allowance and women's rights, had also been a long-time chastiser of Osbert Peake, Under-Secretary of the Home Office whose White Paper, *Civilian Internees of Enemy Nationality*, would lead to the release of thousands of internees by the end of the year. Interning people who were already refugees fleeing from persecution by the very regimes that they were now suspected they might be helping – that Jews might suddenly have become sympathetic to the Nazis – was a theory that no one had so far bothered to question. That was about to change. In August 1940, 1,687 enemy aliens were released from camps and by October, some 5,000 Italians and Germans had been freed. By December, 8,000 internees had been released, leaving around 19,000 still interned in the UK, Canada and Australia. By March 1941, 12,500 internees had been released, rising to over 17,500 in August. By 1942, fewer than 5,000 remained interned, mainly on the Isle of Man where plays and concert parties were staged – many of the internees were writers, artists, actors and musicians – and farm work undertaken. Meanwhile, from 1940 onwards, many of those released had chosen to work on the war effort on the Home Front, or even serve in the armed forces.

Aliens were not the only people who found themselves interned on the Isle of Man. At the outbreak of the war, Sir Oswald Mosley's British Union of Fascists (BUF) – founded by him in 1933 after he had been well received by both Hitler and Mussolini – were considered more a nuisance than a threat. The German blitzkrieg into France and the Low Countries in the spring of 1940 changed all that. On 23 May, a large number of uniformed and plain-clothes officers from Scotland Yard raided the BUF's headquarters in Great Smith Street, Westminster. Mosley was not there but that afternoon five police officers were waiting for him when he returned to his flat in Grosvenor Street SW1. His home, Savoy Farm at Denham in Buckinghamshire, was also searched. Mosley and many others were arrested under new powers which Defence Regulation 18B conferred on the home secretary, Sir John Anderson. A number of his followers were eventually moved to the camps on the Isle of Man where they were segregated from those interned as enemy aliens. Mosley, though, was kept in Brixton prison where he remained until December 1941 when he was reunited with his second wife, Lady Diana, who was in Holloway prison. There they lived in 'married quarters' – a small house with a garden inside the prison walls – until November 1943 and their release on grounds of Sir Oswald's health. The Mosleys were placed under house arrest for the remainder of the war.

Chapter Thirteen

Any Old Iron – or Aluminium?

'The need is instant. The call is urgent. Our expectations are high.'
Lord Beaverbrook

On 10 July 1940, Lord Beaverbrook, the Minister of Aircraft Production, made an impassioned plea for the people of Britain to hand over their aluminium so that it could be made into the fighter planes and bomber planes needed to defend the country against Hitler:

'Give us your aluminium. We want it now. New and old, of every description, and all of it. We will turn it into Spitfires and Hurricanes, Blenheims and Wellingtons. I ask, therefore, that everyone who has pots and pans, kettles, vacuum cleaners, hat-pegs, coat-hangers, shoe trees, bathroom fitting and household ornaments, cigarette boxes, or any other articles made wholly, or in part, of aluminium should hand them over at once to the local headquarters of the Women's Voluntary Services. The need is instant. The call is urgent. Our expectations are high.'

The following day, Lady Reading, founder and chairman of the Women's Voluntary Services (WVS) broadcast her own appeal, 'Remember too, it is the little things that count – it was the little boats that made the evacuation of Dunkirk possible.' The August edition of the *WVS Bulletin* reported on the response:

'Lord Beaverbrook wrote to the chairman: "I send you my warmest thanks for the magnificent work which your organisation is doing in the collection of aluminium pots and pans. I have been most impressed by the energetic and efficient way in which the task is being organised, and I hope you will convey to your assistants this expression of my admiration and gratitude".'

The result of the appeal had been overwhelming. Salvage depots staffed by volunteers were set up in empty shops across the country, and in response to the 'Pans into Planes' slogan – and to catchy headlines like the one in the *Daily Sketch*, 'From The Frying Pan Into The Spitfire!' – the housewives of Britain rushed to the 1,600 dumps hastily organised by the WVS. They brought every conceivable item, many no doubt never dreamed of by Lord Beaverbrook. To a dump in Chelsea someone delivered a racing car with an aluminium body. Piles of artificial legs appeared. One woman parted with her only hot water bottle on the condition that it would be used to help make a Spitfire, not a Hurricane. From what she had read the newspapers Spitfires were superior.

The *Manchester Evening News* explained why there was a shortage of aluminium. It needed the raw material bauxite and France, now under Hitler's heel, supplied perhaps 50 per cent of the world production of that mineral. The United States could not help because they produced only half of their normal peacetime needs. The newspaper said, '… the housewives of Britain are given a great chance to play an important part in winning the war.'

On 16 July, Mrs G.W. Baldwin wrote to the *Staffordshire Sentinel* to say that in only five days she had collected almost enough aluminium to build a Spitfire, which she suggested should be named 'Wolstanton' in honour of the women of that village on the outskirts of Newcastle-under-Lyme who had given so readily. Mrs Baldwin had received a letter from Lord Beaverbrook in which he pointed out that rolled aluminium was required and that was why pots and pans, which were made of that quality, were so important. Mrs Baldwin said that she now proposed to collect the 25,000 pieces of aluminium required to make a bomber.

However, on the day of Beaverbrook's plea to the nation's housewives, the *Daily Herald* had asked, 'When the war is over, the time will come to ask what vested interest held up our aluminium production, and so forced the government thus to appeal for supplies at the present hour of need.'

The situation certainly seemed confusing. According to the *Daily Mirror*, there was plenty of aluminium lying around, but no one wanted it. The newspaper reported that aluminium goods were still plentiful in the shops and that scrap dealers could not find a market for their stock.

Thomas Wilson, the owner of Derwent Brass Works at Swalwell-on-Tyne, said that he had 10 tons of aluminium in his yard and could not find a buyer. He told the *Mirror*:

'When I heard the appeal I was dumbfounded. I know that other metal merchants up and down the country have the same tale to tell. I want to sell 10 tons of aluminium I have here. It would equal a few thousand of the pots and pans that Lord Beaverbrook is asking for.'

George Leech, owner of Nash's motor-breaking yard in Newcastle-upon-Tyne, said that when he heard Lord Beaverbrook's appeal he burst out laughing. He had more than five tons of aluminium in his yard and had been trying to sell it for weeks. Mr Leech, who broke up an average of ten cars a week, all containing aluminium, said that on 26 June he had received a letter from Jebb Brothers, a local firm to whom he sold his scrap. They told him that the bottom had fallen out of the market for aluminium and, consequently, they could not quote for buying his. After hearing Lord Beaverbrook's appeal he had contacted Jebb Brothers again but they had told him the same story; they still could not quote.

Shopkeepers certainly had plenty of pots and pans. Geoffrey Collins, manager of the London-based Aluminium Equipment Company, said, 'Not one of the manufacturers was allowed to make pots and pans after the war began. The stocks of such household goods must have been made before.' The *Daily Mirror* brought all this to the attention of the Hon Geoffrey Cunliffe, Controller of Aluminium. He said, 'I am interested to hear of these difficulties. If the men concerned will get in touch with me then I will give the matter my immediate attention.'

The *Birmingham Daily Gazette* raised a different concern:

'Lord Beaverbrook's intimate and vivid appeal for all and every kind of aluminium article will, by reason of its personal appeal, bring forth a mighty response proportionately greater than the Ministry of Supply's dilatory and, until lately, uncoordinated appeal for scrap generally. It is discouraging to the public to see heaps of scrap iron accumulated weeks ago still lying uncollected, and in this respect the Office of Works seems to be only half doing its job. Then again, there has arisen a campaign for taking down street lamps although, because of the unrelated efforts of Mr Morrison and Sir John Reith, thousands of Belisha beacons still clutter our roads.'

Earlier in 1940, there had been an appeal for iron to help make steel for the war effort. Throughout the country, iron railings were disappearing from buildings both public and private. Newspapers carried photographs of lorries being loaded, and cinema newsreels showed the same scenes. But there seemed to be no images of lorryloads of iron being delivered to steelworks, although that might have been simply to avoid revealing the location of those works to the Luftwaffe, assuming the unlikely event that they did not already know. It has been conjectured that far more iron – some of it, such as wrought-iron, unsuitable for steelmaking anyway – was collected than was ever needed and that most if it found its way into landfills or was even dumped into the English Channel, which would have been a dangerous business in wartime. Some people conclude that the entire initiative was nothing more than an effort to keep up the nation's spirits in the belief that it was 'doing something' after the evacuation of troops from Dunkirk. It has been claimed that only one-quarter of the iron collected was ever used to manufacture munitions and that after the war public records documents on the matter were shredded.

Chapter Fourteen

The Day the Phoney War Ended

'The sky is absolutely patterned with bursts of machine-gun fire ...
the sea is covered in smoke.'

Charles Gardner, BBC

On the still summer's evening of Sunday, 14 July 1940, listeners to
the BBC's Home Service began to realise that the Phoney War really
was over. That afternoon, the BBC had sent reporter Charles Gardner
to Dover where he and his crew set up their recording equipment in a
house overlooking the port before settling down to watch shipping in the
English Channel. Their brief was to see whether the Luftwaffe would
appear; Hermann Goering's new tactic was to launch attacks on British
convoys in the Channel in the hope that this would lure out the RAF
to defend the ships. If heavy losses could be inflicted on Spitfires and
Hurricanes, then Germany's domination of the skies would open up the
path to the invasion of Britain. While Air Vice-Marshal Keith Park, the
head of 11 Group, Fighter Command, refused to be drawn into losing
large numbers of aircraft and pilots over the sea, vital convoys still needed
protecting and modest numbers of fighters still had to be deployed. Thus,
on 14 July, the little BBC party settled down to see what would happen.

Gardner had already witnessed war in the air in 1940. He had spent
time with RAF pilots stationed in France and had been on hand at first
light on 13 May to describe how Flight Lieutenant Lionel Pilkington,
Pilot Officer R.F. 'Dickie' Martin and Pilot Officer D.S. 'Don' Scott
shared a kill, a Dornier Do 17. Now he watched and waited as a convoy,
codenamed 'Bread', continued its westbound journey through the
Channel towards the Dover Straits. The convoy had already been attacked
during the previous few days after the Luftwaffe spotted it making steady
progress between Dungeness and Dover. Spitfires and Hurricanes had
engaged the Dornier bombers and their Messerschmitt Bf 109s and Bf

10s fighter escort. In the *New York Herald Tribune*, Frank R. Kelley (who in the 1960s would win an Emmy award for his part in NBC's coverage of the Apollo space flights) wrote:

'Day-long sallies by waves of German bombers against coastal objectives in England, Wales and Scotland reached a grand climax yesterday in the greatest and fiercest battle of this ten-and-a-half months of war when seventy-five Nazi bombers escorted by forty-five or more fighters roared across the English Channel in two formations and showered bombs on a strongly defended convoy bringing vital food and other supplies to these besieged islands.'

Over the following three days, the Luftwaffe attack on 'Bread' continued and the progress of the air battles could be witnessed along the south coast, which is why Gardner found himself, microphone in hand, looking over the port of Dover at 3pm on 14 July as the convoy of merchant ships with Royal Navy escort vessels slipped into sight. Suddenly the skies above him began to fill with the sound of aircraft. Gardner abandoned his prepared script and began to record:

'Well, now the Germans are dive-bombing a convoy out at sea … there are one, two, three, four, five, six, seven German dive-bombers, Junkers 87s. There's one going down on its target now … Bomb! No! He missed the ships. It hasn't hit a single ship … there, you can hear our anti-aircraft going at them then now … I can't see anything … No! We thought we had got a German one at the top then, but now the British fighters are coming in … you can hear our guns going like anything now … I can hear machine-gun fire but I can't see our Spitfires. They must be somewhere there.'

In fact it was not Spitfires but three Hurricanes from 615 Squadron – they were already patrolling the convoy – that had engaged the enemy. Gardner continued his commentary, apparently enjoying what he was witnessing. He became especially excited when he described what he said was a Junkers crashing into the sea after one of its crew had bailed out. But the doomed aircraft was a Hurricane and the man on the end of the parachute was 24-year-old RAF Pilot Officer Michael Mudie, who had stood no chance of evading the pack of Me109s that had swooped down on him. Although picked out of the sea by the Royal Navy, Mudie was severely injured and died in hospital the following day.

Meanwhile, Gardner went on describing, in unabated joy, the events unfolding before him:

> 'Oh, we have just hit another Messerschmitt. Oh, that was beautiful! He's coming right down … Oh boy! That was really grand … Bomb! Bomb!… Oh boy! I've never seen anything so good as this! Go on, George, you've got 'im.'

Gardner's unedited report, which was just over seven minutes long, was broadcast that evening on the 9pm news programme, in between the Prime Minister talking about the 'War of the Unknown Warrior' and J.B. Priestley speaking about his journey to a deserted and ghostly resort (it was Margate, later termed by the *Daily Telegraph* as 'a now depopulated seaside area of unconcealed identity' described during a broadcast that would itself be highly criticised because it revealed information that might be useful to the enemy).

But for now the nation listened to Gardner's astonishing account, almost mesmerised. What Winston Churchill had already described as the Battle of Britain was being brought directly into their living rooms. '… And there he goes. SMASH! A terrific column of water …' To some this caused great offence. Many listeners regarded Gardner's style – almost as though he was commentating on an exciting football match rather than on an air battle where men were dying – as distasteful in the extreme.

Across the country, horrified people put pen to paper. Writing to the *Daily Telegraph*, Marion M. West of London NW3 commented, '… the BBC's recorded account of an air battle off the south-east coast must have made painful listening to many. Surely the war is not a fit subject to be thus dealt with in the manner of a sporting commentary?' George Manning-Sanders of Cornwall described the broadcast as 'ill-advised', while J.K. Mellor of Herne Hill asked to what public end, other than that of entertainment, had Gardner's report served:

'In the first place it is questionable whether a life–or–death struggle should be treated as a sporting event; and in the next place it is questionable whether the non–combatant public may not be encouraged to do exactly what they have been exhorted not to do – to neglect to take cover in order to watch the progress of an air-raid.'

R.H. Dawkins of Dalston Vicarage, Carlisle, wrote to *The Times*:

'As a pilot in the last war will you allow me to record my protest against the eye-witness account of the air fight over the Straits of Dover given by the BBC in the news on Sunday evening, 14 July? Some of the details were bad enough; but far more revolting was the spirit in which these details were given to the public. Where men's lives are concerned, must we be treated to a running commentary on a level with an account of the Grand National or a cup final? Does the BBC imagine that the spirit of the nation is to be fortified by gloating over the grimmer details of fighting?'

On 19 July, *The Dover Express and East Kent News*, under the headline 'Broadcasting to Germany: That Air Raid Running Commentary', raised another issue:

'The running commentary of an air battle off the south-east coast last Sunday has led to many criticisms of its bad taste. Other criticisms deal with the fact that in their control of the Press, the Ministry of Information forbid publication of details as to where air-raids take place, a rule ignored in this BBC broadcast ... At a time when all sorts of restrictions are being imposed on bona fide residents of coastal areas, there ought to be no facilities for correspondents whose one idea is to get as much past the censor as they can. The BBC's selection of matter from Parliamentary debates and questions also often contains matter that should not be told to Germany. When will this sort of thing be stopped? "Careless Talk" and "Silent Column" propaganda is simply negative by the BBC's attitude. The broadcast by Mr Priestley, in which he described what was happening in Margate, was another breach of the regulations.'

When it came to the gung-ho tone of Gardner's broadcast, not everyone agreed with his critics. On 19 July, the BBC canvassed the opinion of 220 honorary local correspondents (LCs), and a group of industrial welfare workers (WWs) 'recommended by the secretary of their professional society as being likely to report especially intelligently on the radio reactions of large groups of manual workers'.

By midday on Tuesday, 23 July, 166 completed replies (76 per cent of those sent out) had been received from local correspondents and 30 (75 per cent of those sent out) from welfare workers. The report said that it was plain that the broadcast had aroused enormous interest:

'Not a single correspondent or welfare worker said that he or she had not heard the subject discussed, and the vast majority made it plain that spontaneous comment had persisted for several days. A number of correspondents, especially those in factories, say that it was the only topic of conversation on Monday morning and that it was exhilarating to have something real to talk about instead of rumours.'

To the question of whether they thought that the broadcast was widely appreciated or widely disliked, replies were grouped into six classifications:

Widespread appreciation and no criticism: 109 LCs, 20 WWs

Widespread appreciation but some criticism: 36 LCs, 6 WWs

Equal appreciation and criticism: 9 LCs, 3 WWs

Widespread criticism but some appreciation: 3 LCs, 0 WWs

Widespread criticism and no appreciation: 3 LCs, 0 WWs

Appreciation at the time followed by disquiet on reflection: 6 LCs, 1 WW.

A number of replies said that the realism of the account did much to restore faith in the standard news reports 'of one British plane being the equal of a greater number of German planes', while personal opinions seemed to have nothing to do with external circumstances, such as class, age, or relatives in the RAF. They were just personal. Two former airmen who had fought in the First World War disliked the style very much. Several correspondents said that they would not miss such broadcasts for anything, but they realised that the broadcasts might, with good reason, hurt others. Some added that they were ashamed of their own appreciation.

A report compiled by *The Listener* summarised the findings:

'There can be no doubt that this broadcast was enormously appreciated, that it gave a great fillip to morale, (though there is no evidence that morale was in any way shaky beforehand), and that most correspondents believe that the public would welcome more such items if broadcast.

'There is an appreciable amount of feeling that the "football style" was only justified, if at all, by its complete spontaneity i.e. a policy of treating war as a sport would be asking for trouble. The replies of the welfare workers suggest that a large proportion of responsible and sensitive people do not like this sort of thing, contemplated in cold blood, but that as their blood does not run cold in war they appreciate broadcasts of this kind, however much they despise themselves for doing so.

'Judged from the point of view of effect on morale the broadcast was thoroughly justified, but this success does not necessarily mean that further exactly similar broadcasts would be equally successful, partly because the law of diminishing returns is bound to operate, and partly because doubts will arise if commentaries are confined to successful battles.

'With that caution, the evidence is overwhelming that the appetite for first-hand accounts that are known not to be doctored is enormous, and the presentation of good material in first-hand forms is a superb tonic for morale. This conclusion may be linked with the evidence obtained on "Postscripts", which showed how much more popular were first-hand accounts of fact than any amount of the best generalisation.'

An appendix extracted also typified points of view that the investigation had brought to light that all the men and women in workshops agreed that on the Monday the broadcast was the main topic for discussion.

A headmaster in Scotland said:

'I approve very strongly as I have confidence in the members of the BBC staff responsible for such broadcasts. I find that it acted as a real tonic to many people and gave them something to talk about which created a much more healthy atmosphere than the baseless rumours which are commonly discussed. There is no denying that people will talk, so give them something good to talk about.'

'This commentary did more to dispel gloom and the idea of German supremacy than all the talks so far broadcast with the object of keeping up our morale,' said the chief engineer of a radio relay company in East Anglia.

A Midlands working-class housewife agreed. 'It may go a long way to clear the doubt from a lot of people's minds about our pilots taking on the odds they are doing, as quite a few think the reports are cooked.'

'On two occasions recently bombs were dropped on civilians in this vicinity and people were saying, "Where are our fighters?" as there were no signs of them. Such broadcasts can be used by some of us to answer such questions,' was the opinion of an Edinburgh businessman.

A West Riding farmer said, 'The young folk clamour for such programmes ... but the people who suffer from such items need consideration, for their objection is real whilst those who enjoy it are those who enjoy it as a piece of programme full of reality and interest,'

A woman schoolteacher had mixed feelings. 'The commentary caught me unawares and I was fascinated and thrilled by it – but I hated it all the same.'

Although having his own reservations, the labour manager of aircraft equipment factory reported that the general effect on the workforce was excellent:

'Having personally witnessed combats and viewed the remains and bodies, to me the broadcast caused a slight nausea. The description for public entertainment of brave men going to their doom at the instant of occurrence did not appeal to me, but nevertheless gave some unwholesome satisfaction.'

The medical officer at a large chemical works agreed, and showed some cynicism:

'There is little doubt that a certain section of the public would be stimulated by an occasional broadcast of this type. I feel, however, that even for these people broadcasts of this type would soon lose their "morale-raising" value particularly as it became realised that only favourable episodes were so broadcast.'

In a letter to *The Times*, Frederick Ogilvie, the BBC's director-general, defended its decision:

'... This broadcast gave an eye-witness account of an air-action – successful and without loss of British aircraft [not true: Pilot Officer Michael Mudie had lost his life when his Hurricane crashed] against enemy attack on a convoy. The business of news broadcasting is to bring home to the whole public what is happening in the world, and at a grim time like this to play some part in maintaining civilian morale ... People in all walks of life have assured us that they found it heartening and a tonic. One group of fifteen listeners voted it "the finest thing the BBC has ever done" ... It would be a bad day for listeners – that is for the great mass of ordinary people in this the country faced at the moment with all the monotony and anxiety of waiting – if the BBC stood, out of deference to the gravity of the situation with bowed head and arms reversed.'

One could not unconditionally condemn Charles Gardner, who had been thrust into a situation that few civilians had thus far encountered, although one would have thought that having already witnessed air battles over France, while he might mistake a Hurricane for a Spitfire, confusing an RAF fighter with a Junkers Ju 87 – a Stuka dive-bomber – was less forgivable, even in the heat of battle. Later that year, Gardner joined the RAF. After the war he returned to the BBC, before working in the aircraft industry. He died in 1983. For better or for worse, his reaction on that Sunday afternoon was immediate and he had brought war right into the nation's homes. After 14 July 1940, no one could be in doubt that the Battle of Britain had begun.

Chapter Fifteen

Their Finest Hour

'I always think I was lucky because during the war we lived in Kent, right under the Battle of Britain.'

Len Johnson, London

The *Daily Express* of 14 August 1940 told a charming story. The previous day, two women, Mrs Betty Tylee and Miss Jean Smithson, had been the first to reach a young Luftwaffe pilot after his Messerschmitt had been shot down. He asked if they were going to shoot him. 'No,' said Mrs Tylee, 'We don't do that sort of thing in England. Would you like a cup of tea?' 'Yes, please,' said the airman.

In contrast, the newspaper also carried a story about a funeral that took place as an air-battle raged in the sky over the churchyard. The pallbearers wore RAF uniform and an RAF chaplain conducted the service. As the coffin was lowered into the grave one of the Luftwaffe aircraft was hit and fell in black smoke. The coffin contained the body of a young German airman whose own aircraft had been brought down four days earlier. These were just two accounts of what life could be like, living under the Battle of Britain.

It was 18 June when the British people first heard the term 'the Battle of Britain'. That day, evening newspapers across the United Kingdom carried the headline in reporting Winston Churchill's rousing speech to the House of Commons. The Prime Minister had risen at 3.49pm to summarise the war situation. He sat down at 4.25pm after ending:

'What General Weygand called the battle of France is over. I expect that the battle of Britain is about to begin. Upon this battle depends the survival of Christian civilisation. Upon it depends our own British life and the long continuity of our institutions and our Empire. The whole fury and might of the enemy must very soon be turned on us. Hitler knows that he will have to break us in this island or lose the war. If we can stand up to him all Europe may be free, and the life of the world may move forward into broad, sunlit uplands; but if we fail then the whole world, including the United States, and all that we have known and cared for, will sink into the abyss of a new dark age made more sinister, and perhaps more prolonged, by the lights of a perverted science. Let us therefore brace ourselves to our duty and so bear ourselves that if the British Commonwealth and Empire lasts for a thousand years men will still say: "This was their finest hour."'

Four days later, France surrendered and Hitler turned his attention to Britain. Attacks on shipping in the English Channel were followed by raids on RAF airfields and on towns along the coast. On 20 August, Churchill was to make yet another historic speech to the Commons, telling the House, 'Never in the field of human conflict was so much owed by so many to so few.' In those few words, Churchill encapsulated the huge significance of what was happening in the skies over south-eastern England where young pilots – their average age was 20 – took on superior numbers of German aircraft. The previous month, 640 RAF fighters had faced 2,600 Luftwaffe aircraft. At the end of the Battle of Britain, which is generally regarded as having taken place between 10 July – the same day that Lord Beaverbrook was launching his appeal for aluminium to help build fighter aircraft for the RAF – and 31 October 1940, 544 RAF Fighter Command pilots – 15 other nations besides Britain had supplied pilots including many from the Commonwealth, Poland and even the neutral United States and Ireland – had lost their lives, and 1,023 aircraft were lost. RAF pilots claimed to have shot down around 2,600 German aircraft although a Luftwaffe document captured at the end of the war suggests that the actual German losses were around 2,200. Nevertheless, there is no doubt that the RAF shot down many more German aircraft than it lost, thanks to a number of advantages. The Spitfire and the Hurricane were undoubtedly superior aircraft. Under the Dowding System – named for Sir Hugh Dowding, its commander-in-chief – Fighter Command was well organised into different regions so that each could effectively defend its area with a combination of technology, ground defences such as anti-aircraft batteries and the Observer Corps, and fighter aircraft; RAF pilots who survived being shot down could soon be flying another aircraft whereas Luftwaffe pilots were generally captured or ended up in the sea; the RAF could stay in air longer whereas the Luftwaffe had to get back to its bases in France before aircraft ran out of fuel. British factories were also better at quickly repairing damaged aircraft and were also turning out new machines at a faster rate than their German counterparts.

On 13 August, Germany launched a massive attack when wave after wave of bombers carried out ten hours of raids on Kent, Sussex, Hampshire and Essex. The Germans called it *Aldertag* ('Eagle Day') with 1,485 sorties. The RAF responded with 727 sorties. Two days later, the Luftwaffe flew over 2,000 sorties – its targets now covered from Kent to East Yorkshire as well as a large air battle off the Firth of Forth – and lost 75 aircraft; the RAF flew 974 daytime sorties and lost 34 aircraft. On 30 August, the RAF's 1,054 sorties was its biggest daily number so far, against 1,345 by the Luftwaffe. The following day, Fighter Command suffered its heaviest losses of the entire Battle of Britain with 39 aircraft shot down and 14 pilots killed.

On 15 September, the Luftwaffe launched another massive attack in a bid to finally shatter Fighter Command, but the RAF's operational pilot strength was at its highest since the beginning of the Battle of Britain, while production of new fighters had gained even more momentum. That day, the Luftwaffe suffered its biggest losses since 18 August. It was a decisive moment. The Germans had failed to gain air supremacy. Moreover, they did not have command of the English Channel, something that was obviously crucial to an amphibious attack. On 17 September, Hitler's planned invasion of Britain – Operation Sea Lion – was postponed again.

The Battle of Britain changed the mood in the country. There was a new kind of patriotism, more classless than the 'for King, Country and Empire' patriotism of the First World War. People now felt as if they were all in it together. Children especially were thrilled by the dogfights they witnessed overhead. In 1978, Len Johnson of London looked back:

'I always think I was lucky because during the war we lived in Kent, right under the Battle of Britain. That might sound strange if it came from an adult, but were just kids. I suppose we spent more time searching around bombsites, and places where aircraft had crashed, than anywhere else. In the long summer holidays it was great fun. We used to collect shrapnel and anything else we could find and swap it for other things like sweets – which were obviously in short supply – or perhaps even a football, if you had enough "currency". Because that is what all these spoils of war were – currency. Sometimes, you'd just swap what you had for a "better" bit of shrapnel to build up your collection. One day my brother was setting off for work and I was still in bed, and he called up to me that a German plane had been damaged that night and that part of its engine was lying in our front garden. I'd never moved so fast. I got dressed as quickly as I could and raced downstairs. There was no sign of anything in our garden, though. He was pulling my leg. That was the thing, though – we lived right in the thick of it and we just made a joke of it all. It was just part of our lives.'

So the Battle of Britain had been won and Hitler's plans to invade had been frustrated, but now a change of tactics meant that British resolve and togetherness was about to be tested to the limit.

Chapter Sixteen

The Sky Was Lit Up by Searchlights

'After a cup of tea, things didn't seem so bad. Sadly, I lost four sisters and two little nieces in the Christmas Blitz that followed.'

Phyllis Essex

In August 1940, Pulitzer Prize-winning journalist Ray Sprigle was in England to report on the war and to see just how Britain was keeping calm and carrying on. That August, filing a story from 'the South-West Front', Sprigle told of an experience he underwent when the air-raid siren sounded as he slept in his hotel. He stumbled down to the air-raid shelter, to find that he was the first to arrive. It was, wrote Sprigle, a 'de-luxe' shelter with white-topped tables set out in an adjoining room that also contained a piano. One by one, the other guests came in, quite calmly, and sat around while the manager's wife poured them tea as the raid went on overhead. Eventually one guest, uninvited, began to play the piano, with one finger, knocking out probably the only tune he knew.

'Wouldn't it be grand if Jerry dropped a bomb on him?' said another guest. That did not daunt the player, but then one lad in the corner decided to compete by doing impressions of a cat and dog fight and a hen laying an egg. Then everyone started singing, first *South of the Border* and then *The Last Roundup*.

The hotel manager told Sprigle him that he recently visited a friend. He arrived to find the friend picking through the wreckage of the family home. When the previous air-raid had started, the man had put his wife, two daughters and the family's two pet dogs under the stairs, while he and his small son sheltered in the sitting room. A bomb had come straight down the chimney.

The man said that he had shaken his arms and legs and 'as none fell off, I figured I was all right' and then he extracted his wife, daughters and dogs from under the stairs that had collapsed on top of them. Remarkably, none of the family was seriously injured. As they emerged into the street, an old man was walking past. He stopped to survey the wreckage of a pub on the corner that had also suffered a direct hit.

'Hell of thing,' said the old man, 'when an Englishman can't get his dram or his beer because of that blighter in Berlin.'

'All over England,' wrote Sprigle, 'people are taking these air-raids in their stride ...'

Would they continue to do that as the bombing intensified? Sprigle had no way of knowing just what concentrated terrors were about to be unleashed upon the civilian population. Until now, air-raids had been unpredictable and sporadic, mostly aimed at military targets and often carried out by single aircraft that newspapers took to describing as 'a lone raider'. People had expected Neville Chamberlain's announcement on 3 September 1939 to be followed by wave after wave of German bombers. They had seen cinema newsreels of what had happened to the Poles. But for the British, nothing much happened immediately and then, when it did, only slowly before, in the late summer of 1940, the Blitz began. It had been the same in towns and cities all over Britain.

The warning siren that had sent Derby's citizens scurrying to their shelters on the first night of the war had been a precaution until aircraft over the eastern counties had been identified. The first enemy aircraft did not arrive in the vicinity until early December, when a Heinkel reconnaissance was spotted. It was not until 25 June 1940 that the first bombs fell on the town that was home to a Rolls-Royce aero engine factory that manufactured Merlin engines for the Spitfires and Hurricanes that were about to fight the Battle of Britain. That June night, Derby suffered its first civilian casualty of the war when 67-year-old Elizabeth Evans died at her home in Violet Street, a mile and a half from the Rolls-Royce works.

On the day after the raid, the 'Candid Column' of the *Derby Evening Telegraph* criticised the behaviour of some people in the aftermath of an air-raid. Presumably, columnist 'The Sage' was referring to events in Derby itself, although wartime censorship generally prevented Luftwaffe targets from being immediately identified:

'Incidents in the air-raid over a Midlands town yesterday morning, as described to me by people close to the scene of action, were frightening, funny, or just plain foolish. Curiosity will be the death of many before this war is over, despite the fact that for nearly a year the authorities have dinned into our ears good advice on what to do and what not to do during an air-raid. People feel that they must look out; and others have an even more dangerous urge to go out.

'I am assured that at one spot in the Midlands where bombs were dropped and a woman was injured, hardly a quarter of an hour had passed before there were sightseers prowling the street to discover and to inspect the craters which the bombs made. That was an hour or more before the "raiders passed" signal was given.

'There are services arranged to deal with the distressed and injured, so there is no excuse for Tom, Dick and Harry, and their wives, to crowd into a stricken area for that purpose. There is nothing clever in being first on the spot; and there is no particular value in pieces of metal simply because they once formed part of a bomb ...'

'The Sage' also had something to say to say about people who chose to listen to the radio during an air-raid:

'... the wireless can be an infernal nuisance during an air-raid alarm. It may sooth some nerves but it frays others to the raw. Nobody objects to a man or woman choosing music to give them a bit of Dutch courage to ease the tension ... but why on earth some people think it necessary to assume a mood of forced merriment, turn on their sets at full blast and twiddle the knobs incessantly is beyond explanation ... The Government will have to do something about these radio fiends ere long for the sake of public order and sanity, not to mention the folk who have to get some sleep.'

One can only imagine that 'The Sage' had a troublesome neighbour.

In the 25 June raid on Derby, two houses were also destroyed in the suburb of Mickleover where, when a bomb fell in a neighbouring garden, 39-year-old Elsie Henson was hit in the head, chest and legs by splinters as she made for her air-raid shelter. Her husband, Hugo, and their 7-year-old daughter, Hazel, had not left the house and were uninjured although their home was badly damaged. Six days after the raid, Mrs Henson died of her injuries in the nearby Derby City Hospital. By August, with air-raid sirens sounding almost nightly, police had to prevent frightened Derbeians from camping out in their shelters. On 14 August, 70-year-old Margaret Hutton was killed at her home in Hawthorn Street, adjacent to the Rolls-Royce factory. Medical personnel from the aero-engine works rushed to help but were unable to save her. Five days later, an overnight four-hour raid left three dead, also in the town's industrial heartland: Annie Andrews, who was 69, died on her way to the Derbyshire Royal Infirmary; 42-year-old Doris Bentley and her 17-year-old daughter, Sheila, both died in hospital the day after the raid. The *Derby Evening Telegraph* could only report of an air-raid 'on a Midlands town' although an accompanying photograph showed bomb damage to the instantly recognisable home of Derby County. The caption described it simply as 'a famous Midlands football ground'.

Derbeians were now getting a taste of what the war would really be like. Alec McWilliams recalled standing on high ground in the suburb of Littleover and seeing the distant south-western sky red as blood as fires raged in Birmingham and Coventry, while overhead German bombers droned north towards Sheffield and Manchester because, of course, Derby was not the first industrial town to be bombed. That unwanted distinction had fallen to Middlesbrough where, on 24 May 1940, at just before 2am, a bomb fell near North Ormesby. As the single aircraft flew in a corridor over South Bank and Grangetown, it dropped twelve more bombs. At the Dorman Long steelworks, eight workers were injured, three of whom – John Bidwell (42), Trevor Evans (46), and Jonathan Jones (19 – were admitted to hospital. A young girl was slightly injured by a bomb splinter but was treated at the scene.

The *North Eastern Gazette* reported that many people had, remarkably, managed to sleep through the raid. Mrs L. Walkington said:

'We dashed out to our brick shelter and suddenly remembered that our 10-year-old daughter, Margaret, was left in the small bedroom. My husband ran back and found her fast asleep although the bed was covered with broken glass and splintered woodwork. She had wakened but had dropped off to sleep again, quite unworried. Every back bedroom was littered with glass. It was awful, but the amazing thing is that no one was cut or hurt and everyone was calm.'

One man, awakened by the sound of the first explosion, 'went out and inspected the crater with the idea of finding souvenirs'. On his way home he found that another bomb had fallen on allotments near his home. Another man said, 'When the bombing began we all made a rush for our shelters but the plane passed over and away so quickly that we did not bother to take cover. We went round to see what damage had been done and were surprised to see so little.' Apart from the bomb on the allotments, another had fallen on a disused building. A woman who lived close by said, 'I jumped out of bed and ran to the window. The sky was lit up by searchlights and I clearly saw a plane caught in the beams. The anti-aircraft guns were also firing.'

The residents of one street had a narrow escape when a bomb fell near their back doors. The walls, doors, outhouses and sculleries were blown in and every window and frame smashed, but a brick-built outhouse almost on the spot was not penetrated. Mrs J. Spoul, who kept a small confectionery business in the street, at the rear of which one bomb fell, expressed the view that as it had landed on the soft earth covering an air-raid shelter and not on the stone pavement, 'the street was saved from a much worse fate'. The ARP chief for the district said, 'There was no panic – the spirit of the people was one of fierce determination and their behaviour was splendid.' On the same night, bombs fell in rural areas of East Anglia with 'slight damage to two cottages' and a cow and a pony were killed. A bomb dropped on Essex and killed some chickens, and two heifers were injured when a bomb fell at the rear of a farmhouse.

Newcastle's first taste of a major air-raid came on 2 July 1940. The Luftwaffe's target was the High Level Bridge that spanned the River Tyne between Newcastle and Gateshead. Thirteen people were killed and 123 injured that night. On 15 August, German bombers flying from airfields in Denmark and Norway again dropped bombs on Newcastle and this time also on Sunderland where Wearside shipyards produced one-quarter of Britain's merchant shipping. The following day, the

Sunderland Echo had no reservations about naming the target. Not for them the usual 'North-East town'; under the headline 'Sunderland Raid Incidents' it reported:

'Many Sunderland families owe their lives to Anderson shelters. In yesterday's mass air-raid large numbers of people in shelters as near as a yard to bomb craters escaped unhurt.

'Casualties were providentially small. An air-raid warden on duty was killed. Three other persons who declined an invitation to share a neighbour's shelter were also killed. Not a single person in a shelter was, so far as is known, injured. Seaham Harbour was also bombed by the Nazi armada of 100 bombers escorted by fifty fighters which carried out the North-East coast raid. Casualties were on a rather heavier scale than in Sunderland ... John Henderson, an air-raid warden, was fatally injured by shrapnel while on duty. It was Henderson's first day on duty as a part-time warden.

'Three people were killed in one house on a main road after they refused to take shelter. A man, a woman and a little girl were seated at the foot of a flight of stairs when a bomb crashed through the roof and burst only a few yards from them, inflicting fatal injuries. "We had just finished dinner when the siren went," said Mr Robert Miller. "I wanted them to come down to the shelter, but they said they would be alright in the house. I left them sitting at the foot of the stairs ..."'

Sunderland's pre-war England international footballer Raich Carter, now serving in the in the Auxiliary Fire Service (AFS), was one who braved the bombing, on one occasion risking his life on what turned out to be a fool's errand. After an incendiary bomb hit the Binns department store in Sunderland, Carter was one of dozens of firemen sent to tackle the blaze. When he arrived, flames were shooting from one side of the street to the other. It was dirty, dangerous work and eventually the firemen were ordered to withdraw. First, though, Carter and a colleague were sent back into the building to retrieve a precious length of hose. The two men made their way up several flights of stairs, burning embers falling on them, sheets of flame running up the walls, their lungs choked by smoke. Carter felt they should abandon the hunt for the hose, but his colleague pressed on before being beaten back by the flames. He collapsed and Carter had to bring him down over his shoulder, stair-by-stair, finally staggering into the cold night air, lungs bursting. Bent over, head between his legs, gasping for breath, Carter was told that the hose had not been left in the building after all. Another fireman had brought it down with him and dumped it in a yard. When Carter was promoted to the full-time brigade, the local newspaper received a number of letters accusing the council of favouritism in selecting him out of 240 applicants. The criticism irritated the player who, with his full-time colleagues, was working long and dangerous hours.

Meanwhile, the *Newcastle Weekly Chronicle* carried some valuable advice about 'how to behave during an air-raid':

'Remember, when you are suddenly awakened, especially by an alarm, the whole of your system is relatively dormant, the blood is not circulating so rapidly or widely. If you jump up hurriedly you put a strain upon the blood system and, of course, the nervous system. You get out of balance ... lie still for a moment or two. Get thoroughly awake on your back – not on your feet. You will feel much fitter and better than in the early days when you "jumped to it" too violently. Now, once in the air-raid shelter, relax as completely as you can. Remember you can do nothing unless something does happen in your immediate area ... If you can get off to sleep, so much the better. If you must talk, get away from war talk. After the raid get off to sleep as quickly as possible and don't worry about another raid. Time enough to do that when it comes ... Don't forget that none of you stay at home lest you are run down by a car. Yet your chances of being killed on the road in normal times are greater than being killed by a bomb in wartime. In short, do everything well but deliberately and RELAX, RELAX, RELAX.'

In Hull, the first air-raid siren had also sounded in the small hours of Monday, 4 September 1939. It, too, was a false alarm, as were those that followed until the last alert of the year, on 21 November. Thereafter, the city's ARP committee continued to meet every day except Sunday. As

Christmas came and went, and well into early summer, there were no more sirens. Then, on 19 June 1940, at just after 11pm, an incendiary bomb was dropped on the Marfleet district, near the King George Dock. Just over an hour later, incendiaries and high-explosive (HE) bombs fell on East Hull, on Victor Street and Buckingham Street, but relatively little damage was done compared to how the city would eventually suffer.

Two weeks later, on 1 July, East Hull was one of two targets – the small Scottish town of Wick was the other – for the Luftwaffe's first daylight raids on mainland Britain. A lone aircraft went apparently undetected until it opened fire at around 5.30pm. Oil tanks at Saltend, 5 miles east of Hull, were set on fire when pieces of bomb shrapnel pierced a tank that held 2,500 tons of petrol. The fuel spilled out, threatening other tanks. As petrol was drawn off and tanks cooled with foam it was a night for great bravery. Five George Medals were awarded to men who prevented a major disaster. Two Hull firemen, Jack Owen and Clifford Turner, together with three members of staff at the plant, George Howe, George Sewell and William Sigsworth, were honoured with the medal that would be instituted on 24 September 1940 by George VI.

In October, Hull had its first taste of parachute mines. There were two fatalities. A woman setting off to the shops was turned back by an ARP warden who told her that he had just found a human ear in the road. There were non-fatal casualties, too, and extensive damage to hundreds of houses. Yet by the end of November 1940, Hull had not fared too badly. Indeed, on 3 August the *Hull Daily Mail* reported:

> 'Yesterday Hull received a great deal of notice in the national Press because of Thursday's visit of the king and queen. It will be unfortunate if, as a result, relatives of Hull people get the impression that the city is badly damaged, or that we are in such a state of depression that we need some special recognition to keep our spirits up. We who live here and traverse the streets day after day know that this is far from the truth … we are not in any need of a tonic.'

It was the seemingly unending alerts and consequent sleepless nights that were putting people on edge. On 12 December, however, they had much more to worry about than the loss of a few hours' sleep. The first explosive incendiaries were dropped, and as winter tightened its grip, firemen faced a new hazard when water from their hoses spilled on to streets and froze so that men lost their footing as they tried to control the hoses. Fireman who rowed out in small boats to douse fires on barges in the middle of St Peter's Dock found their hoses so frozen that they had to be carried back to be thawed at fire stations across the city.

On Christmas Eve came the first real taste of the horrors to come when a warehouse in one of the oldest parts of Hull and containing 6,500 tons of grain and castor beans was hit. Floor after floor collapsed, fire hoses were buried under burning debris and in the tight, narrow streets firemen faced the constant danger of falling walls. Even after the fire was brought under control, it had to be watched for days afterwards lest glowing embers helped to guide the next wave of German bombers.

Hull had already prepared for the challenge. In the summer of 1940, air-raid wardens set up a scheme where furnished houses were made available to bombed-out families until they could sort out their own accommodation. Initially twenty-one empty houses were equipped with essentials – beds, chairs, tables, cooking utensils and crockery, coal, and even tea and sugar – all thanks to the generosity of the wardens, their families and friends. While men saw to repairs and maintenance, women lit fires and had a pot of tea on the table for the next occupants. They became known as 'the Good Companions'. By the end of 1940, the Ministry of Health had given the scheme its official blessing and 200 such houses were available to the victims of the Blitz. Priority was given to pregnant women and families with children.

By the end of the war, Hull could count itself one of the most heavily bombed cities in the United Kingdom. Indeed, according to the *Yorkshire Post*, Hull was the most devastated city in the UK per square mile, but a government notice preventing its naming for reasons of national security was lifted only in the 1970s. More than 1,200 of its citizens were killed, some 3,000 injured. Out of the city's 91,000 houses, 5,300 were totally destroyed and a further 3,000 severely damaged. It is estimated that, overall, 91 per cent of its housing stock was damaged in some way or other and over 152,000 people rendered homeless. In some city-centre streets, few buildings had been left standing. In 2017, it was reckoned that 1,213 high explosives, 101 anti-personnel devices and 70 incendiary explosives were still buried under the streets, gardens and allotments of Hull.

Unexploded bombs were now an ever-present danger in most towns and cities. On 18 September 1940, under the headline '"We Want Your Bombs" Is Their Heroic Motto', the *Birmingham Daily Gazette* reported on the men of the Royal Engineers' bomb disposal sections:

'Early in the raiding season the Midland Region had three of these sections under the command of Lieutenant D.S.F. Rayner, formerly a Territorial, whose home is in Birmingham. It was a party of his men, in the charge of Sergeant [William] Bodsworth of Thorpe Street Drill Hall, Birmingham, who investigated a small hole in a field near Redditch. The hole was believed to contain a delayed-action bomb and, as it had been there for three days, it could be expected to blow up at any moment. The sappers nevertheless dug down in search of the bomb, found it at last, about 20ft below the ground, and heard its clockwork fuse still ticking. It was a 500lb bomb, so anyone may guess what would have happened to Sergeant Bodsworth and his party if the bomb had done its worst at that moment ...'

The area's 9th Bomb Disposal Company lost almost forty officers and men during the war. On 24 November 1940 alone, they were faced with no less than 305 unexploded bombs still awaiting their attention. Their bravery was inestimable. When 42-year-old Second Lieutenant Alexander Campbell was called to deal with an unexploded bomb at the Triumph Engineering Company's works in Coventry, he found the device was fitted with an irremovable delayed action fuse. While the bomb was being transported from the factory where it had landed to a less populated area, Campbell lay alongside it, listening for any sound that it had become active so that he might alert the driver and give him the chance to jump out of his cab and run for cover. Campbell defused the bomb safely but the following day, Friday, 18 October 1940, he was killed by another bomb that he and his colleagues had transported out of Coventry's city centre to a safe area. They had just unloaded the bomb when it exploded, also killing Sergeant Michael Gibson (34) and Sappers William Gibson (22), Richard Gilchrest (23), Jack Plumb (25), Ronald Skelton (20), Ernest Stote (21) and their driver, Ernest Taylor (32), of the Royal Army Service Corps. Campbell and Michael Gibson were each posthumously awarded the George Cross. Gibson's award was for his actions a month earlier when he had heard an unusual hissing noise coming from an unexploded bomb and sent his men away before defusing it alone. Their story is but one example of many heroic of acts performed by bomb disposal units, although sometimes with comical asides.

G.A. Shapland told this story:

'It was during the Blitz on London in 1940 and a stick of bombs had fallen in Pembridge Crescent, Notting Hill Gate, and failed to go off – UXBs we called them.

'It was thought that one had penetrated the sewer – a brick one about 30ft deep – and the bomb disposal sergeant said that he would remove it. I asked him how he would get it out and he said he would go into the sewer, tie a rope to the bomb and pull it out, so I gave him a safety-lamp to use and then he said: "Oh, by the way, are there any rats down there?" And when I said: "Yes", he said: "Well, I'm not going down there, then. We'll dig for it instead." And he made his men dig a hole 30ft deep and got the bomb like that. He was prepared to face an unexploded bomb – but not a rat!'

Bravery in the Blitz came in many forms, though. The *Birmingham Daily Gazette* told of heroics during a raid on the city on the night of 25–26 August 1940:

'No George Cross citation makes more graphic reading than the story of heroism told in Birmingham yesterday when two RSPCA officials, Miss Marion E. Almond and Mr Maurice Jones, received the Society's highest award, the Margaret Wheatley Cross and Certificate, for rescue work during one of the city's heaviest raids. On duty at an RSPCA hospital, they had, over many hours, extinguished some sixty incendiaries with the aid of Mr Jones's brother, and rendered first-aid to firemen and other people when, it was stated, the position became "nearly desperate". With premises burning fiercely all around, they decided that the creatures – all evacuees from bombed homes – could stay no longer. So seventeen cats, eight dogs and a canary, all in terrified condition, were loaded into an ambulance and taken out of town to other kennels and pens. So difficult was the four-mile journey that it occupied two hours and at many points they were allowed by the police to proceed only at their own risk.'

In September, the same newspaper told the story of a 'Birmingham hello girl commended for her pluck' during a raid the previous month. Miss Winifred Gilhooly, who lived in West Bromwich, had just completed a twelve-hour shift as a Civil Defence telephone operator but, when there was no one to replace her, she insisted on carrying on through the night. She was awarded the King's Commendation. 'It was a hazardous night, for bombs fell quite close; nevertheless, she carried on with exemplary efficiency.'

In the early days of 1940 there were some humorous moments, too. Mrs E. R. Smith of West Bromwich recalled:

'One late spring night the first air-raid warning sounded in Smethwick. At the time I was newly married. My husband was in the armed forces and I was living in rooms with a very old and very deaf lady. I was in bed and, since it was a very warm night, I was wearing no nightdress. 'However, at the sound of the siren, I jumped out of bed and ran to the old lady's bedroom shouting: "Mrs B, the air-raids have started! The sirens are going!" She, poor soul, being very deaf, said "What?" I said, "The bulls are blowing!" The "bulls" were the pre-war factory sirens telling everyone it was time to go to work. With that, panic-stricken and, I am afraid, cowardly, I ran downstairs, grabbed a coat and a pair of sandals and raced to the nearest shelter, which was down a steep hill in the local park. On my flight I tripped and cut my knee. Reaching the shelter, which was dark and empty, I stood there trembling for what seemed like hours but could have been no more than 5 minutes, when a man and two small children entered. I spoke. He nearly jumped out of his skin; he thought I was a ghost. I told him that I'd fallen, and with the aid of a match – in the circumstances I was glad he'd no torch – he bound my knee with a clean handkerchief. A few minutes later, more terrified people came in and my 'Sir Galahad' said he would take me to the first-aid post when the all-clear sounded. There the first-aid officer dressed my knee and I managed to hold my coat together this time. When he took me home, we found that poor Mrs B had barricaded herself in her room. When she peeked out of the window and caught sight of the first-aider still wearing his helmet, she panicked. "The Germans have got her! Please don't have me, I'm only an old woman!"

'The first-aider was an old neighbour and knew Mrs B well, and realised there was no point in him trying to calm her, so ran down the street to fetch her son. After some difficulty, Mrs B's son managed to get to his mother, who clearly still thought she was in the hands of the Germans, and was yelling and crying. Only when she saw her daughter-in-law did she calm down. I didn't stay much longer with Mrs B, but I reckon I was the first air-raid casualty in Smethwick.'

Birmingham's first major air-raid of the war took place on 9 August 1940 when one person was killed when a single aircraft dropped its bombs on Erdington. Four days later, the Castle Bromwich Aircraft Factory – where in June production of Spitfires had begun – was attacked. Eleven bombs fell on the works, killing seven people and injuring forty-one. It was a sign of things to come; between 19 and 28 November some 800 people were killed – 53 of them workers at the Birmingham Small Arms (BSA) factory when more than 400 tons of HE bombs were dropped on the city in one raid – and 2,345 were injured and 20,000 made homeless. Birmingham's longest air-raid of the war took place on 11 December 1940 when the city was under attack for thirteen hours.

Late in 1940, the name of Coventry became synonymous with the Blitz. Between August and October there were several small raids on the city, altogether killing 176 people and injuring almost 700. But on the evening of Friday, 14 November came the worst of all. The attack by 515 Luftwaffe bombers, code-named *Mondscheinsonate* (*Moonlight Sonata*), was intended to destroy Coventry's industrial infrastructure. Over the next few hours of a brilliant, moonlit night an estimated 568 people – the exact number has never been established – were killed and more than 850 seriously injured. The death toll would have been far higher had not many citizens, after previous air-raids, decided to leave to sleep in nearby villages. More than 43,000 homes, just over half of Coventry's housing stock, were damaged or destroyed and some two-thirds of the city's other buildings damaged, among them the great mediaeval church of St Michael where only the tower, spire, outer wall and the tomb of its first bishop remained. It was to be the only English cathedral largely destroyed in the Second World War. The central library and market hall, hundreds of shops and public building and sixteenth-century Palace Yard, where James II had once held court, were also destroyed.

In all the Luftwaffe had dropped 500 tons of high explosive, 36,000 incendiaries and 50 landmines on Coventry. It was also trying out a new weapon, the exploding incendiary. The eleven-hour raid traumatised the city. Hundreds of dazed people wandered the streets and there were reports of children trying hopelessly to burrow their way through brick walls in a bid to escape the terror.

Newspapers generally referred only to attacks on unnamed towns and cities, identifying them only by their broad location, even though it was obvious to readers that the air-raid had been on them. This time there was no point in hiding what had been done. Although the following day's Coventry-based *Midland Daily Telegraph* still led its front page with 'Berlin Gets Biggest-Ever Bombing', its second story was 'Coventry Bombed: Casualties 1,000'. A Ministry of Home Security communiqué reported that 'the scale of the raid was comparable with those of the largest night attacks on London', before claiming that 'the enemy were heavily engaged by intensive AA fire which kept them at a great height and hindered accurate bombing of industrial targets'. In fact almost one-third of Coventry's factories had been destroyed. Another third were severely damaged. Yet, thanks to the use of 'shadow factories' outside the city and the rapid repair of less damaged works, production was resumed relatively quickly. Because Coventry's shops had been bombed there were major food shortages and while the regional commissioner, the Earl of Dudley, brought in troops to help clear debris from bomb-shattered streets, local people were helping out by providing food and blankets. One woman drove around in a car, handing out bread and other provisions, and mobile canteens were brought in. On 16 November, the king visited Coventry. Alderman John Moseley had been made the city's mayor only five days earlier and the council's initial reaction was they were not ready to entertain such an important guest, but after an exchange of telephone calls with Buckingham Palace the visit went ahead. The *Coventry Evening Telegraph* said:

> 'No king was ever more a man among his people than King George VI when he came to Coventry ... and for four hours made Coventry's sorrows his own. It may be that never in the whole history of the British monarchy has a royal visit proved more of a tonic to a suffering people – nor left behind more inspiration for the gigantic task of restoring order out of chaos. The king walked for miles around the shattered districts of the city ...'

Industrial cities and major ports were obviously going to be the main targets of the Luftwaffe. In August 1940, German reconnaissance flights had been seen over Sheffield, world-famous for its steel making and now a major centre of arms production. In two raids, on the clear, moonlit, frosty nights of 12–15 and 15–16 December, almost 700 people were killed. Although damage to industrial areas was relatively light – the Neepsend Gas Works was the worst affected – Sheffield's city centre was devastated with nearly 3,000 homes and shops destroyed. The two raids killed 668 civilians and 25 servicemen, injured 1,500, and left 40,000 homeless. A communal grave in the City Road Cemetery received 134 victims. Seventy bodies were recovered from the Marples Hotel that received a direct hit at just before midnight on 12 December. The final death toll was never established but, miraculously, seven men were found alive in the hotel basement.

One man who died was George Lawrence, a local benefactor who owned a razor blade factory in Sheffield. He left the safety of his home in the Derbyshire countryside to drive into the burning city to take food and drink – including four bottles of whisky that he picked up from a local pub on the way – to his workers, despite being told several times by police officers that he should turn back. He was one of eight people who died when his factory took a direct hit.

Seven months after the first raid, the *Sheffield Star* reported that the bodies of four people killed that night had been found under a pile of debris. Jessie Hill (16), Beatrice Hawksworth (26), Percy Smith (26) and James McLardy were apparently all sheltering in a passageway between two houses when it collapsed. Some victims were never found. At 4.15pm on 12 December, 18-year-old shop assistant Sylvia Redfern left her home to go to the Central Picture House. That evening the cinema was destroyed. Sylvia was never seen again. Juggler Edward Kerford was in the middle of his act at the Empire Theatre when the raid started. As bombs fell on the city, together with his partner, Roy Billam, he sheltered under the stage. At about 11pm Kerford decided to walk back to his theatrical lodgings, telling Billam, 'It's quieter now. I think I'll make a break for it and get home to the digs. See you in the morning.' The following day, after Kerford had failed to appear, Billam went to the St Mary's Road digs to find all the houses flattened. Five bodies had been recovered but two of them were unidentifiable. Kerford's wife, Nora, requested an inquest and also placed an advertisement in *The Stage* magazine asking for any information regarding her husband's whereabouts. She received no response and the coroner pronounced her husband dead, yet another person to have disappeared during the December 1940 Blitz on Sheffield.

There were tales of heroism here, too. Leslie Currie, a sanitation inspector, was one of six men awarded the George Medal for their courage during the Sheffield Blitz. Ignoring the possible collapse of debris, he rescued members of a family trapped in the ruins of their house. Currie was married with a two-week-old daughter.

Addressing his congregation after the second raid, the Bishop of Sheffield, Dr Leslie Hunter, said:

'Sheffield has had a cruel visitation, which has brought into the open the staunch quality of its people. Going around the stricken areas and going into rest centres, one can only admire the patient endurance of the homeless and the readiness of everyone to help as best they can. I am pleased that clergy and other helpers have opened additional rest centres where and when needed. The strain on our resources over the next few days will be great, but if the same spirit is maintained, and all co-operate with those in authority, we shall get through and carry on the service of the nation.'

Sheffield's lord mayor, Councillor Luther Milner, told the city's Emergency Committee:

'I think very few of us contemplated when we met a month ago that we should have to pass through the terrible experiences which have befallen the city ... It has been my sad experience to attend one or two funerals, and I do wish on your behalf to extend to every suffering person in Sheffield our very deepest sympathy.'

Major air-raids on Manchester had started in August and, in September, the Palace Theatre in Oxford Street was bombed. But the heaviest raids on the city took place on consecutive nights, 22–23 and 23–24 December. Many of the city's firemen and Civil Defence workers had still not returned from Liverpool, which had been badly hit on 20 December. In fact, it was the fires that still raged on Merseyside that helped illuminate the bombers' way to Manchester where the Free Trade Hall, St Anne's Church and Smithfield Market were all destroyed and Oxford Road and Deansgate made impassable by unexploded bombs and debris. More than 8,000 homes were destroyed or made uninhabitable and the Trafford Park industrial area, where in 1940 the former Ford factory had reopened to manufacture Rolls-Royce Merlin aero-engines, was also badly damaged. On the night of 23 December, the Metropolitan-Vickers factory at Mosley Road was hit, resulting in the loss of the first 13 Avro Manchester bombers that were in final assembly there.

More than 750 civilians were killed including three generations of the same family celebrating Christmas at a party in Miles Platting. Another party, for first-aid staff, held in the late afternoon rather than the evening because of the threat of raids, had nearly finished at 7.15pm when a bomb landed in the road outside the depot at Eccles, killing eleven people including an ambulance driver, a Red Cross nurse and an air-raid warden. Twenty-four people were killed in Moss Side, including ten who lived at the same address. It was a landmine that destroyed houses in Stretford that caused the biggest single loss of life when thirty people died. More than a dozen members of a wedding party perished when a bomb struck the Manley Arms pub in Hulme. The landlord and his wife, John and Jeanie Rogerson, were among the victims.

During 1940, Merseyside was the most heavily bombed area in Britain outside of London. On 28–29 November, 350 tons of high explosive bombs fell there and from 20–23 December, it was hit on successive nights. Docks were the Luftwaffe's main targets, which meant that the surrounding streets, where many of the dockworkers lived, suffered devastation. Between August and the end of the year there were over fifty raids, in September and October occurring every couple of nights.

On 29 November, about 300 people were taking cover in a large underground shelter in the basement of the Ernest Brown Junior Instructional Centre in Durning Road, Edge Hill. A parachute mine scored a direct hit on the three-storey building, which collapsed into the shelter below. This was actually a boiler room, chosen because it had a reinforced ceiling with girders running across it. Gas escaped from fractured mains, and boiling water from the central heating system poured into the shelter. The fires that raged in the building above made rescue work an extremely hazardous task. The death toll of 166 men, woman and children was the largest single loss of life in the Liverpool Blitz. Winston Churchill described it as 'the worst single civilian incident of the war'.

Phyllis Essex recalled a story from when she was living in Liverpool in 1940:

'It was 6 September. It was the day before I was to be married and I was 38 years old. The air-raid alert sounded at 8pm. My brother, my youngest sister – who was in bad health with TB – and myself all got under the stairs. My mother insisted on going to bed. Her philosophy was that, if your name was on a bomb, you'd get it anyway, and she wasn't prepared to lose sleep over it. Well, sorry to say, that night we got a direct hit on the front of the house. Luckily, it was only a 250lb bomb. But my dear mother was trapped in bed with the roof on top of her. We screamed for help from the ARP wardens and, finally, they got her out alive. She was very shocked and had a bad cut on her forehead. Well, the funny part of it was when the ARP warden said to her: "I can still hear your chimney clock chiming!" she replied: "I only paid thirty shillings for it off a jeweller. He must have been an honest man!" With the neighbours' help we cleaned her up and, after a cup of tea, things didn't seem so bad. Sadly, I lost four sisters and two little nieces in the Christmas Blitz that followed.'

While the North and Midlands were now feeling the full force of the Luftwaffe's new tactic, the South too was suffering. On 8 May 1940, Sir Geoffrey Peto, Civil Defence Commissioner for the South-West, held a press conference in Bristol where he told journalists:

'There has been a feeling that the West will not be bombed first. But that is not the German procedure, which is to go all-out from the start in the same way as they seized the ports of Norway. If the Germans come – and I think that they will, sooner or later – they will attack all-out and the first raid may be the biggest of the lot. They won't give us warning by dropping a few bombs on the East End of London and then gradually move to the West. The West will be in it from the beginning. I don't think that the West realises that.'

Sir Geoffrey appealed to retired people not eligible for the fighting services to join the ARP. The *North Devon Journal* wholeheartedly supported the scheme:

'People have not sufficiently realised the necessity for protecting not only our own homes but also the homes and families of men fighting for us. This is a great responsibility placed on the civil population. The commissioner is right in appealing particularly to retired people and to women to help in ARP duties. In Finland all the ARP work had been done by women. Under the new scheme, cuts will have to be made in paid ARP staff, and so the need for unpaid volunteers will grow. In particular the casualty services need strengthening.'

By November 1940, the citizens of Bristol had endured many air-raids, the city a target because of its industry and position. The Bristol Aeroplane Company, whose wartime headquarters were at Clifton, manufactured the Beaufighter that had several roles, as a ground attack aircraft, night fighter, long-range fighter and torpedo bomber. The city was an easy target as bombers could plot a course from Avonmouth – where the docks were also major targets – up the River Avon to Bristol itself. On 2 November, the Luftwaffe dropped 10,000 HE bombs and 5,000 incendiaries on the old part of Bristol. Three weeks later, 148 bombers dropped 12,000 incendiaries and 160 tons of high explosives. Within the first hour of the raid, over 70 fires were burning. The death toll that night reached 207 and thousands of houses were destroyed. Four of Bristol's ancient churches were badly damaged. The lord mayor, Alderman Thomas Underwood, summed up. 'The City of Churches had in one night become the City of Ruins.' The plan for the raids had been to destroy the port and the aircraft works but it was Bristol's medieval centre that always seemed to bear the brunt of the attacks. In two raids in early December, the city centre was bombed again, killing another 256, among them two AFS firemen. By April 1941, 1,299 Bristolians had been killed, 1,303 seriously injured and 81,830 houses had been completely destroyed.

The presence of a naval base in Portsmouth made that city a prime target. Alerts had sounded before but at around 7am on 11 July 1940, the Luftwaffe finally arrived in numbers overhead. Eighteen people were killed that day and when the bombers returned a month later, the death toll was considerably higher. Then, on 24 August, the people of Portsmouth were given a taste of what was to come. Over 200 bombers attacked the dockyards and surrounding areas, killing 125 and injuring over 300. Eight children perished as they watched a matinee performance at the Princes Theatre in Lake Road. A communications problem meant that no air-raid warning was given. For several hours, German bombers dropped bombs on or around a burning house. A *Portsmouth Evening News* reporter was told that, for some reason, it seemed that the bombers were deliberately attacking the spot. An eyewitness was quoted as saying, 'The ruthless way in which they kept up the attack suggested that they either thought it was a military target, or that they had gone completely mad.'

On 26 August, only the skill and bravery of the RAF pilots of 43, 602 and 615 squadrons, together with cloudy conditions over the Channel, saved Portsmouth from worse damage, other than a direct hit on Hilsea gasworks. The months of September, October and November passed with relatively little damage from further raids but on 5 December, over 40 people died in a city-wide attack. Two days before Christmas another raid left 20 dead and more than 160 injured. In 1941 more than 500 would die in three major air-raids on Portsmouth. The naval dockyards were always the major targets but, inevitably, the city would always suffer too.

Throughout 1940, only occasional small-scale raids hit Plymouth, with its dock and Devonport naval base, although, of course, there were still casualties. The first raid on Plymouth came at around midday on 6 July 1940, when a single aircraft dropped its bombs on a council housing estate at Devonport, killing three people. There was another raid the following day and intermittently thereafter.

On 11 September, thirteen people were killed and fifteen others injured when a bomb fell on the Stonehouse district of the city. Two weeks later, a heavy raid targeted Keynsham Dockyard and ships in Plymouth Sound. Overall, though, the Luftwaffe was reserving the city for a series of devastating raids in 1941, when more than 900 people would be killed and 40,000 made homeless.

As a large city on the south coast, Southampton was always going to be a strategic target for the Luftwaffe. But it was also the home of the Vickers Supermarine factory in the suburb of Woolston, where Spitfires were being built, which made it doubly important as far as the Germans were concerned. The Luftwaffe attacked the riverside factory in daylight raids on 24 and 26 September 1940, when 110 people were killed and much of the works was destroyed. Another daylight raid, on 6 November, targeted the Civic Centre School of Art, which Hermann Goering had said looked like a piece of cake and he was 'going to cut himself a slice'. A 500lb HE scored a direct hit on the building, killing thirty-five people including fourteen children who were having an art lesson in the basement.

Southampton suffered fifty-seven raids overall, the first bombs falling on 20 June 1940, the first major attack coming on 23 September, and the worst on the Saturdays of 23 and 30 November. In the first of these, which lasted from 6.15pm until midnight, 77 people were killed and more than

300 injured, with what was left of the Civic Centre again taking much of the attack. The city was ablaze and German propaganda broadcasts claimed that the glow from the fires could be seen on the French coast at Cherbourg. Among the dead was 48-year-old Edgar Perry, who had survived the sinking of RMS *Titanic* in 1912. He perished when a bomb hit the Garibaldi Arms in Crosshouse Road. Perry's wife, Martha, together with the pub's licensees of just two weeks, Albert and Vera Reynolds, and eleven other seamen were also killed. The licensees' four children survived after taking shelter under the bar when siren sounded.

One week later, the Luftwaffe returned to drop 800 HE bombs on Southampton, killing 137 people, 96 dying in their air-raid shelters during the six-hour raid. Water and gas supplies were cut off and firefighting reinforcements had to be brought in from other areas because the AFS was short of staff. Much of their equipment proved incompatible with that of the local brigade.

For some cities, 1940 ended relatively quietly with no real indication of what the Luftwaffe would unleash the following year. For the first eighteen months of the war, Exeter suffered only twenty raids, mostly by single hit-and-run bombers. On 7 August 1940, a lone raider dropped five bombs on the St Thomas area of the city, causing little damage to property. The Exeter *Express and Echo* reported that one man was injured but managed to walk to a nearby first-aid post and the only other casualties were a canary, which died from shock, and several chickens which were also killed. Again, the report could identify only 'a South-West town' but the accompanying illustrations were credited to one of the newspaper's photographers and, anyway, the location would have been instantly recognisable to any local.

In Wales, the Luftwaffe targeted Cardiff – whose docks made it certainly the biggest coal exporting port in the United Kingdom and probably in the world – on 3, 10 and 12 July, and again on 7 August, after the fall of France put Cardiff within easier range of German bombers, but the heaviest raids would be in 1941. The first raid on Swansea began at 3.30am on 27 June 1940 when bombs were dropped east of the city centre with little damage and no loss of life. For the rest of the year, only single aircraft or very small groups of aircraft targeted Swansea.

Although the heaviest civilian loss of life in Scotland – 1,200 people dead – would come in the March 1941 raid that largely destroyed Clydeside, in 1940 Scots would experience the bitter taste of war on the Home Front. On 1 July, the little Caithness town of Wick suffered a tragedy when fifteen people, eight of them children aged between 5 and 16, were killed when a Junkers 88 flew out of low cloud and dropped two bombs, intended for Wick harbour, on a street in Bank Road, Lower Pultneytown during the school holidays which, because of the war, had that year been extended to last from 18 June to 1 October. On 26 October, three more civilians – two children and a woman – died in Hill Street near the aerodrome at RAF Wick when three Heinkels dropped more than twenty HE bombs during an attack on the base.

While Dundee largely escaped – because, according to local legend, Hitler's granny came from the city – Montrose did not. On October 25 1940, four Norwegian-based Heinkel 111s bombed RAF Montrose, where more than 500 pilots were being trained. Five men were killed and twenty-one were wounded while extensive damage was done to buildings and aircraft. Dundee's worst incident came on 5 November 1940 during what seemed like a random attack. Four bombs fell on the city, one of them killing four people in a four-storey tenement in Rosefield Street. Another bomb narrowly missed the Forest Park Picture House cinema that was packed with children.

In late May 1940, the lord provost of Edinburgh, Henry Steele, at the opening of an AFS fire station in Corstorphine, to the west of the Scottish capital, said, 'If Edinburgh is ever bombed by the German air force, the AFS and the citizens will face that danger bravely.' They did not have long to wait. On 18 July, a 'stray' bomb from a lone German raider killed seven people in Leith. On the same day – Edinburgh's first air-raid of the war – another bomb fell on George Street, killing 17-year-old Jane Rutherford. In Commercial Street, a bomb landed only yards away from a tramcar. It exploded, leaving a huge crater but, amazingly, the twenty passengers on the tram were unhurt. Other raids in July caused damage but no loss of life, but in September a two-storey block was flattened in West Pilton where it took two hours for rescue workers to dig out the body of 7-year-old Ronald McArthur. His 5-year-old sister, Morag, was found lying near him. She died in an ambulance on her way to hospital.

On 7 October, four bombs fell, damaging roofs in Marchmont, and on 4 November two fell on open ground at Edinburgh Zoo.

The first-raid on Aberdeen happened on 26 June 1940 and the city had been expecting it. But when in November a lone German bomber attacked Campbeltown on the Kintyre peninsula, damaging a hotel by the harbour and shattering glass doors at the town's Art Deco cinema, it was yet another seemingly random attack on a small Scottish town that, even as the war elsewhere began to gather in fury, had never expected to find itself a target.

Scotland, though, did see the first civilian to be killed on British soil, and he died a hero. On 16 March 1940, when a bomber returning from a raid on warships anchored at the naval base of Scapa Flow jettisoned its remaining bombs on the Orcadian hamlet of Brig o' Waithe, 27-year-old labourer James Isbister, a father of one, pulled two passers-by inside his home for safety. When a bomb fell on the house opposite, he dashed out to help. Moments later he lay dead, killed by a hail of shrapnel.

Chapter Seventeen

'The Whole Bloody World's on Fire ...'

'You felt you really were walking with death – death in front of you and death hovering in the skies.'

Mea Allan, *Daily Herald* journalist

For many people mention of the Blitz means only one thing – London and that day, 7 September 1940, when Hitler turned his attention away from RAF airfields and focussed instead upon the capital. Like everywhere else in Britain, up to that point Londoners had viewed the air-raid warnings and the blackouts as mostly rather irritating. In a diary now held at the Imperial War Museum, entitled 'Journal Under The Terror', Miss P. Warner described how, after a brief trip to a Fabian Summer School in Devon on Sunday, 1 September 1940, she had returned to London to find the capital 'apparently unchanged in spite of the frequent air-raid warnings. Familiarity has bred contempt and the heart-chilling wail of the siren has been followed so often by a deathly silence that it now means little. The streets remain crowded, lovers wander arm-in-arm, children play their games, men tend their gardens undisturbed'.

On Friday, 6 September, she wrote:

'I attended a Promenade Concert at the Queen's Hall ... and although the warning had gone, the entire hall was packed with a mammoth audience. On to a theatre where a further warning had no effect on a big audience, then to a restaurant jam-packed with jovial beings, and home through streets whizzing with traffic under an impressive display of searchlights.'

For London, as with so many other cities, the first air-raid siren had sounded just a few hours after war was declared. Like all the others it was a false alarm, but by the late summer of 1940, the war was coming much closer to the capital. The Civil Defence Region 5 (London) covered a much wider area than the city itself. On 16 August, there was a heavy raid on the Thames Estuary and 'south-western suburbs of London'. Several people were reported killed when a bomb hit a railway booking office and others died at Tilbury and Northfleet. German news reports claimed that there was a huge explosion in the Purfleet area and that parts of Barking were on fire.

On 22 August, bombs were dropped on Harrow and Wealdstone, causing damage to two cinemas, a dance hall, a bank and some houses, but with no loss of life. Two days later the Luftwaffe returned and this time nine people were killed.

The early August raids on civilians – over the country 1,078 would be killed that month compared to 258 in July – were mostly accidental and the bombs meant for airfields and other military targets. This was certainly the case on Thursday, 15 August when RAF Croydon was attacked. The aerodrome itself was badly damaged with a direct hit on its armoury, training aircraft destroyed and craters pockmarking the airfield. However, the intervention of nine Hurricanes from 111 Squadron meant that the majority of the Messerschmitt Bf 110 twin-engine heavy fighter-bombers dropped their bombs outside the base. Five airmen from 111 Squadron and one from the station headquarters were killed but it was the civilian population that bore the brunt of the raid. Several factories and houses were hit, killing 62 civilians and injuring 185. After the all-clear sounded, dozens of locals peered over the aerodrome fence to look at the damage.

The first raid on the City itself – the 'Square Mile' – came in the early hours of Sunday, 25 August 1940 when bombs fell on Cripplegate. The warning siren – the sixth of the day – had sounded at 11.08pm on the Saturday. One bomb scored a direct hit on the turret of St Giles Without Cripplegate, where a statue of the poet John Milton, who was buried in the church after his death in 1674, was blown off its pedestal but not badly damaged. Buildings in Fore Street were set alight and it took more than 800 firemen and 200 pumps to bring the fires under control. The 'nuisance' raids that had kept Londoners on their toes but still able to go about their daily business were soon to be replaced by concentrated bombing that would go on relentlessly for months.

Saturday, 7 September 1940 – the day after Miss Warner had enjoyed a Beethoven concert followed by the theatre and a nice supper – was 'one of the fairest days of the century' according to William Sansom, the London advertising executive turned full-time firefighter. What he was about to experience would inspire much of his work as a novelist. It was indeed unseasonably warm in London with the temperature in the high 80s as 348 German bombers escorted by 617 fighters took off from northern France. At 4.14pm, the first aircraft were spotted crossing the English coast.

Taking tea in their home at Sissinghurst Castle in the Weald of Kent, the politician and diarist Harold Nicholson and his wife, the writer Vita Sackville-West, watched them coming over in wave after wave. 'There is some fighting above our heads and we hear one or two aeroplanes zoom downwards. They flash like silver gnats above us in the air.'

American journalist Ben Robertson, who was reporting on the war for New York-based daily newspaper *PM*, watched as this aerial armada 'flew at a very great height, glistening like beautiful steel birds in the afternoon sunshine' as it made its way towards London.

The raiders started over the docks and the densely populated East End. At 6.10pm the raid ended. Two hours later, a second wave of bombers, aided by the fires that were now burning, arrived over the capital. The writer and independent MP, A.P. Herbert, who was serving as a petty officer in his own boat, *Water Gypsy*, in the River Emergency Service, witnessed the bombing from the middle of the River Thames. He described the scene below London Bridge as like 'a lake in Hell'. Burning barges drifted everywhere and although he and his crew could hear the 'hiss and roar of conflagration', they could not see it because the smoke was so dense. When they finally reached a dock, they found 250 acres of timber on fire. A fire officer was trying to get the blaze under control. He asked Herbert to get someone to send him more pumps. 'The whole bloody world's on fire!'

That attack lasted until 4.30am on Sunday, 8 September. One bomb fell on a crowded shelter on the Peabody Estate in Whitechapel, killing seventy-eight people including fourteen children. In what was described as 'a million to one chance', the bomb had fallen directly on a 3ft x by 1ft ventilation shaft – the only vulnerable place in a strongly protected underground shelter that could accommodate over 1,000 people. *The Scotsman* reported:

'Children sleeping in perambulators and mothers with babies in the arms were killed. ... The bomb fell just as families from scores of nearby streets were settling down for the night ... Hitler's revenge took a terrible toll among several families. In one, three children were killed. Their parents escaped, grief-stricken. One man, when the smoke and noise had died down, searched for his wife, found her lying on the ground, turned her over. She was dead. Hours afterwards one woman, her head and arm swathed in bandages, was in the refuge room of the shelter waiting for news of her two children. She did not know that both were dead ... Yesterday the shelter presented a tragic picture. Perambulators and corrugated iron sheeting lay entangled. There were heaps of bedclothing and pillows, blackened gas masks, toys and the remains of meals ... ARP and AFS workers said that, despite it all, there was no panic. "The women were magnificent," was the comment on all sides.'

In those first two days, 430 Londoners were killed and more than 1,600 seriously injured. In a letter dated 7 September, Mea Allan, the *Daily Herald* journalist, said, 'You felt you really were walking with death – death in front of you and death hovering in the skies.'

This was just the start of fifty-six out of fifty-seven consecutive nights when an average of 200 bombers a night pounded London.

On 12 September, Harold Nicholson was lunching at the Savoy when the American journalist Hubert Renfro Knickerbocker dashed up to him 'aflame with rage'. He told Nicholson that he had 'the best story in the world and the censors are holding it up'. A delayed-action bomb outside St Paul's Cathedral threatened to go off at any moment. 'Cannot the American people be brought in to share my anxiety?' Knickerbocker wanted to know.

That bomb, which had fallen during a night-time raid and weighed two tons, was buried 30ft in soft soil near a gas main close to the west entrance of St Paul's. It could not be disarmed, and detonating it in situ would have destroyed the cathedral. The only option was to remove it intact. It took a team of bomb disposal sappers three days to dig it out. Once they had exposed the massive bomb they used two lorries to pull it carefully from the ground. They took it to Hackney Marshes where it was detonated, leaving a 100ft-wide crater. Lieutenant Robert Davies, who drove the truck on which it was secured, and Lance-Corporal George Wylie, to whom had fallen the task of actually excavating the bomb and whose 'untiring energy, courage and disregard for danger was an outstanding example to his comrades' were each awarded the George Cross for their bravery.

Although the government had decreed that London Underground stations could not be used to shelter from air-raids, on the night of 19–20 September 1940, thousands of Londoners ignored the ruling. They arrived with bedding, food and flasks of hot drinks. On 21 September, faced with a tide of public revolt that it could not stem, the government removed its objection. Many stations were equipped with bunks, chemical toilets, first-aid posts and canteens.

During the Blitz, an estimated 177,000 people sought refuge in the Tube and countless lives were undoubtedly saved.

On 15 November, the biggest, brightest moon of the month shone down as almost every London borough was hit. Targets included Westminster Abbey, the National Portrait Gallery and Euston railway station. On 29 December came the heaviest raid of them all. Incendiary bombs – 100,000 – were the Luftwaffe's main armament that night and there were 1,500 fires including one that covered half a square mile. Eight Wren churches were destroyed, hospitals and railway stations were hit, and only the walls of the Guildhall remained standing. Thanks to an American reporter cabling his office with the description, the night would become known as the 'Second Great Fire of London'. One photograph stands out as the iconic image of that night, St Paul's Cathedral surrounded by smoke and flames, a picture taken by the *Daily Mail*'s chief photographer Herbert Mason, who was on a roof, on firewatching duty.

The American journalist Ernie Pyle, who in 1944 would win the Pulitzer Prize, described the scene he witnessed from a balcony overlooking the city:

'Into the dark shadowed spaces below us, while we watched, whole batches of incendiary bombs fell ... We saw two dozen go off in two seconds. They flashed terrifically, then quickly simmered down to pin points of dazzling white, burning ferociously... The greatest of all the fires was directly in front of us. Flames seemed to whip hundreds of feet into the air. Pinkish-white smoke ballooned upward in a great cloud, and out of this cloud there gradually took shape – so faintly at first that we weren't sure we saw correctly – the gigantic dome of St Paul's Cathedral.'

Winston Churchill had ordered that St Paul's must be protected at all costs. It would be a crushing blow to the nation's morale if it were lost. As bombs rained down on the cathedral, volunteer firewatchers from the St Paul's Watch – some of them members of the Royal Institute of British Architects – armed with sandbags and water pumps, attempted to douse the flames. The fire brigades had a major problem; water was in short supply because the pressure was already reduced due to demand, now mains were being ruptured by the bombing and although hoses could be filled from the Thames, the river was at an unusually low ebb, not to mention the unexploded bombs that lay in its mud. At about 9pm, an incendiary device lodged on the roof timbers of the great cathedral. As it burned, the lead of the famous dome started to melt. But then the bomb became dislodged, fell to the floor of the Stone Gallery and was smothered with a sandbag. Wren's masterpiece was saved. The words of the American broadcaster Ed Murrow – 'The church that means so much to London is gone. St Paul's Cathedral is burning to the ground as I talk to you now.' – were premature. As Pyle wrote:

'St Paul's was surrounded by fire, but it came through. It stood there in its enormous proportions – growing slowly clearer and clearer, the way objects take shape at dawn. It was like a picture of some miraculous figure that appears before peace-hungry soldiers on a battlefield.'

On this December night, together with his friend, the artist Leonard Rosoman, William Sansom, who wrote of the glorious weather on the first day of the Blitz back in early September, was now fighting a fire in Shoe Lane, off Fleet Street, when Rosoman was relieved of his hose. Moments later a wall collapsed, killing two firefighters, one of whom was the man who had just taken Rosoman's place. The incident haunted Rosoman for the remainder of his life and he immortalised the scene in his painting 'A House Collapsing on Two Firemen, Shoe Lane, London, EC4'.

In all, 14 firemen and 160 civilians died that night, hundreds of buildings were destroyed or badly damaged, streets were covered in rubble from collapsed buildings, tramlines were uprooted and road surfaces spontaneously combusted in the 1,000-degree Centigrade heat. Four days earlier, Harold Nicholson had written in his diary that while 'Paris is so young and gay that she could stand a little battering ... London is a charwoman among capitals and when her teeth fall out she looks ill indeed'.

Air attacks were not restricted to dry land. On 11 January 1940, crowds on the shore watched as the *Smith's Knoll* lightship was attacked by a German bomber off the Norfolk coast. A syndicated newspaper report told readers:

> 'As the men got into the boats the plane machine-gunned them until the boats were riddled. The raider fled when six fighters appeared ... one [survivor] remarked: "We always reckoned that lightships were not fair game and were accustomed to seeing the Jerries pass without worrying us. We never had a chance."'

On 29 January, at 9.30am, the *East Dudgeon* was attacked by a Junkers 88. The crew of eight took to a lifeboat and tried to row across the Wash to the Lincolnshire coast 25 miles away. In the worst winter weather for decades, their craft capsized on a sandbar and only one man, John Sanders from Great Yarmouth, survived. He told newspapers:

> 'We were not alarmed because on previous occasions the Germans had waved to us and left us alone. But on this occasion the bomber dived suddenly and sprayed the deck with machine-bullets and dropped nine bombs. The ship heeled and seemed to go right under.'

The Germans claimed that the *East Dudgeon* was a naval patrol vessel. So far as the Luftwaffe was concerned, lightships were now fair game. The following month, the Transport and General Workers' Union demanded that both the First Lord of the Admiralty, Winston Churchill, and the Elder Brethren of Trinity House provided lightships with 'the proper means of defending themselves' against such 'cruel and dastardly attacks on these unprotected men'. Churchill told the House of Commons that lightships had 'always been regarded by civilised nations as outside the scope of bombing'.

On 12 February, Prime Minister Neville Chamberlain announced that lightships were to be protected and that, where possible, in outer positions light floats would replace them. Chamberlain denounced the killing of lightship crews as 'not war, but murder', using the *East Dudgeon* attack to characterise the enemy that Britain was facing:

'Such acts of pure gangsterism have little, if any, practical effect on the outcome of the war ... the horror and disgust which they excite in the minds of all decent people only makes us more resolved to carry on the struggle until civilisation is purged of such wickedness.'

Later in 1940, cinema audiences watched *Men of the Lightship*, when the attack of the *East Dudgeon* was the subject of a short propaganda film produced by the Crown Film Unit for the Ministry of Information. In the film, the ship's crew comprised real lightsmen rather than professional actors.

By the end of 1940, several more lightships had been attacked. On 14 August, the *Folkestone Gate* was sunk and two of its crew lost. On 25 October, the *South Goodwin* lightship was bombed and sunk. On 1 November, the *East Ouse* was sunk with the loss of six of its crew. The *Cromer Knoll* 25 miles off the Norfolk coast, and the *Nore,* at the mouth of the Thames Estuary, were also attacked and, by the end of the war, twenty-seven lightsmen had been killed and twenty lightships lost.

German bombs killed more than 43,000 British civilians during the Second World War, almost half of that number in London alone. Before the end of 1940 there were 55,000 casualties of one sort or another. By the time the Blitz on Britain had ended, two million houses had been damaged or destroyed, 60 per cent of those in London where more than 70,000 buildings were completely demolished. In the capital, rescue services responded to 16,396 incidents with 22,238 people extracted from bomb-damaged premises.

On land or sea, though, how did Britain deal with months of bombing? Invoking what would one day come to be known as the 'Blitz Spirit' where the British faced with great fortitude every horror that the Luftwaffe could visit upon them, in November 1940 the Southampton-based *Southern Daily Echo* reported that 'these people survive today amazingly cheerful, and full of courage'. Yet a Mass Observation survey taken on 4 December recorded that the people of Southampton were 'broken in spirit' and that from 4.30pm in the afternoon there was a steady stream of people leaving the city to sleep in the New Forest and outlying areas, something that came to be called 'trekking' – travelling out of the city in the evening and returning in the morning. The survey said that many people were trying to hitch lifts out of Southampton to escape the bombing and that there were also people who pinned notes to their back doors saying that they would be 'back tomorrow'.

This seems less a case of low morale and more a rational response to a very real danger. It would be the 1970s before the survey would be released – to be met by fierce protests – and in 1974 another released document, the Hodsoll Report, compiled at the time by the Inspector-General of Air-raid Precaution Services, Sir John Hodsoll, also provoked local anger when it claimed that an incompetent civic administration in Southampton had been incapable of dealing with the aftermath of the bombing.

Whether the Blitz Spirit is a myth or was a reality, it seems that it sometimes depended on where you lived. Studies show that, for instance, while in Bristol morale had been low – the main dissatisfaction there being with the provision of air-raid shelters – in Liverpool, morale was high, probably because, unlike Bristol, damage had not been concentrated on the city centre. There were suggestions, too, that Liverpool's place as a major seafaring city also helped it weather the worst of times because sailors were a particularly jolly bunch. A Mass Observation report claimed that 'morale in Liverpool is appreciably higher than in any other blitzed town observed so far'. There were accounts of 'good humour and laughter ... singing and whistling ... Nowhere have we seen more drunkenness, more singing and cat-calling, more picking up or more people being sick ...' than in the centre of Liverpool after dark, where it was also felt that because sailors' wives were used to long periods living alone, it stood them in good stead 'compared to the wives of Coventry munitions workers or Cockney bus conductors'. More than anything, though, as Mass Observation noted, 'Liverpool has not had to stand the test of one concentrated blitz on one area of the town'.

By contrast, Mass Observation found that after the raid of 14–15 November 1940 in Coventry, where the city centre had been almost razed to the ground, there was:

'an unprecedented dislocation and depression ... There were more open signs of hysteria, terror, neurosis observed in one evening than during the whole of the last two months together in all areas. Women are seen to cry, scream, to tremble all over, to faint in the street, to attack firemen. The overwhelming dominant feeling on Friday was the feeling of utter helplessness ... In two cases people were fighting to get on to cars, which they thought would take them out into the country, though, in fact, as the drivers insisted, the cars were just going up the road to the garage'.

In fact, the report had been compiled only two days after one of the most devastating air-raids on Britain during the entire war. There was little wonder that people there felt dislocated and depressed and that they were telling the Mass Observation volunteers that 'Coventry is finished'. It should also be mentioned that interviewees had 'admiration for the ARP and AFS services' and that there were 'very few grumbles'. One week after the raid, Mass Observation found that morale in Coventry 'is of the highest order'.

A report referring to the raids on Manchester over 22–26 December 1940, said that people there were 'definitely on edge, are afraid of the next raid, are really beginning to worry about the future ... the morale of the bombed largely depends on the care they get in the first 36 hours'.

Angus Calder, author of *The Myth of the Blitz*, theorised that what appeared to be high morale was nothing more than a 'grim willingness to carry on'. Most people had no other choice. They had emerged from the difficult 1930s with its high unemployment and class barriers and the working class at least bore the worst of the bombing because they lived near the factories and docks where they earned their living and which were now being bombed. Psychoanalysts had expected mass nervous breakdowns due to the bombing of civilians but, in fact, the special clinics opened to receive an anticipated high number of mental casualties were closed down because there was no need of them. Instead, family bonds became closer and instead of increasing, the number of suicides and cases of drunkenness declined.

The way that the Royal Family conducted themselves throughout the Blitz also helped bind the nation. The king and queen spent most of their days at Buckingham Palace before retiring to Windsor Castle in the evenings. The palace was hit several times. On 8 September 1940 – that dreadful day on which seventy-eight people had been killed on the Peabody Estate in Whitechapel – a 50kg delayed-action HE bomb landed in the palace grounds. The following day, another fell near a swimming pool. When the bomb was detonated it destroyed much of the pool and there was damage to the north wing of the palace. On Friday, 13 September came the raid that was to give Londoners the lasting belief that their monarch really was sharing their ordeal. There were three daylight raids on London that day. It was during the second of these, at around 11am, that a bomber specifically targeted Buckingham Palace with a stick of five HE bombs. A court correspondent was leaving the palace as the attack started:

> '... a twin-engined plane was seen diving from the clouds ... the pilot appeared to cut his engines and the machine lost speed. Then came the whistle of bombs, and explosions were heard in rapid succession ...'

Two bombs hit the inner quadrangle, rupturing a water main and shattering hundreds of windows on the southern and western sides. One bomb struck the Royal Chapel in the south wing. Four workmen were hurt and taken to Westminster Hospital where one of them, Alfred Davies, died of his injuries. The chapel was destroyed.

Another bomb fell on the forecourt, and one in the road between the palace and the Victoria Memorial. That was detonated the following morning, leaving a crater 30ft by 20ft by 10ft deep. Two days later, the *New York Herald Tribune* reported:

'The belief that the German air attack on Buckingham Palace was a deliberate attempt on the lives of King George VI and Queen Elizabeth was great in force today as expressions of horror and disgust poured in from all over the empire. The rails and stone lamp pillars in front of the palace were hurled down when a time bomb dropped in a recent raid exploded this morning with terrific force, hurling debris over the forecourt and the memorial to Queen Victoria, and gouging a deep crater in the sidewalk.'

The king and queen were in residence at the time of the raid. After the all-clear sounded, at about 1.30pm, they visited East and West Ham. Later that day, the queen wrote to her mother-in-law, Queen Mary. She described how she felt as though she was 'walking in a dead city ... all the houses evacuated, and yet through the broken windows one saw all the poor little possessions, photographs, beds, just as they were left'. She famously remarked, 'I am glad we have been bombed. It makes me feel I can look the East End in the face.'

That day's evening newspapers told the story in detail, reporting on the 'Nazi murder raider' and the 'barbarous attack' on the king and queen. In a broadcast to America, the journalist Raymond Gram Swing described the bombing of Buckingham Palace as:

'a great psychological blunder ... The king and queen were in the basement like the rest of London ... their home was hit and they emerged to speak quietly, bravely and unselfishly to those injured. Tonight Britain is more unified than before that German bomber slid down over Buckingham Palace. Now they all have shared this ordeal, king, queen and everyone else. They are one.'

On Sunday, 15 September, bombs hit the palace lawns and the Regency Bathroom facing the West Terrace. In the skies above the palace, Sergeant-Pilot Ray Holmes, out of ammunition, flew his Hurricane directly into the tail of a Dornier Do17. The bomber crashed on to a tobacconist's shop near the forecourt of Victoria Station. Its pilot, who had bailed out, landed near Vauxhall Bridge and was set upon by a crowd of locals. He died of his injuries the following day, at Queen Alexandra's Military Hospital in Millbank.

Holmes's Hurricane came down at Ebury Bridge on Buckingham Palace Road, while Holmes, from 504 (County of Nottingham) Squadron that had been scrambled from Hendon, parachuted to safety, landing on a slate roof in Hugh Street before sliding down into a garden. Not surprisingly, his welcome back to terra firma was in sharp contrast to that of the Dornier pilot. He told reporters, 'Two girls came to me and saw that I was an RAF man. I was so glad to see them that I kissed them both.' Locals led him to the nearby Orange Brewery pub on Pimlico Road where he drank brandy before being taken to Chelsea Barracks. After a medical examination and a few more drinks in the mess, Holmes, who had worked as a crime reporter on Merseyside before the war, was put into a taxi and driven back to RAF Hendon. In 2004, archaeologists recovered the Merlin engine from his crashed Hurricane.

Holmes may have saved Buckingham Palace from further damage that morning but two days later a delayed-action bomb landed near the Royal Apartments. It was detonated around 7pm with minimal damage to property. On 16 October, a parachute mine landed in St James's Park, blowing in windows at Buckingham Palace, and on 1 November, a bomb hit the palace lawns, damaging windows and a ground-floor bedroom. The Royal Mews was also damaged.

Despite all the horrors of the Blitz, some people saw a funny side, albeit sometimes years afterwards. Mrs W.M. Shaw told the story of an air-raid as she was tending to her new-born son at Forest Gate Maternity Hospital in east London in October 1940:

'I had to stay there nearly three months, as I'd been very ill through kidney trouble while I was expecting my first baby. I had an uncanny knack of hearing the bombs coming down before anyone else, so I used to tell everybody to duck under the bedclothes. Well, I eventually had my baby boy on 9 October at 11.30am. About an hour and a half later, at dinnertime, there was a raid with no warning sirens. The nurse was just going to get my baby for me to feed him, when I heard a bomb falling and shouted everyone to duck. I did so myself and, thank God I did, for when it was all over I emerged from under my bedclothes I couldn't believe it. My bed was covered in glass. Even the window frame was on the bed. I stuck my head through it and said: "I think I've been framed!"'

Eileen Godfrey recalled an incident when Ilford was bombed:

'Our neighbours had been offered an Anderson shelter in 1938, but had refused. By September 1940, the London Blitz had begun and they changed their minds. By this time, however, the demand for shelters was high and they had to wait. In the meantime, they dug the hole, ready for the delivery of the shelter and we took some palings out of our fence to enable them to use our shelter. One night there was a particularly heavy raid. We were already in the shelter when Mrs McC came down in her nightdress with a thick eiderdown wrapped around her. When I tell you that Mrs McC was around 14st, you'll know that we weren't surprised when she got wedged in the shelter entrance. Her husband, Jack, began to push her from the rear, as we were pulling her from inside. Suddenly she fell in head first, leaving the eiderdown wedged in the entrance. Fortunately, she wasn't hurt and we all had a good laugh.

'After a while, Mrs McC asked where the gas masks were. Jack said he hadn't got them and that they must still be on the kitchen table. Jack was a silly old fool said Mrs McC, and he'd better fetch them "before we were all gassed to death". So Jack went inside to fetch the masks.

'We heard a terrific crash, followed by a few muffled choice words, then another crash, followed by Jack falling headfirst down into the shelter. He'd put on his gas mask in the house and, of course, couldn't see where he was going. He fell down the hole he'd dug for his own shelter, hit his head on the crossbeam of the fence and knocked the snout of the gasmask upwards and sideways so as it finished somewhere above the region of his left ear. He never heard the end of that.'

Chapter Eighteen

More Heroes of the Blitz

'No one realises the damage a bomb can do until they see it …'
Rose Ede, 17-year-old recipient
of the George Medal

On 17 October 1940, a German mine fell through the roof of a house in Shoreditch, East London. The mine failed to explode and Sub-Lieutenant Jack Easton (34) and Ordinary Seaman Bennett Southwell (27) were sent to deal with it. With the area evacuated, and the mine in an awkward position, they attempted to defuse it in situ. Easton began work with Southwell passing him tools. Suddenly the bomb starting ticking. Both men fled. Easton dived for cover but Southwell kept on running down the street. The explosion destroyed a large area of housing. Easton survived, eventually freed from a huge pile of rubble, but Southwell, who had started work in bomb disposal only a month earlier, caught the full force of the blast and was killed. Both men were awarded the George Cross.

Sub-Lieutenant John Babington (29) of the Royal Naval Volunteer Reserve was awarded the George Cross when he climbed into a 16ft-deep pit made by a German mine at Chatham Dockyard in September 1940. He defused it, despite knowing that it was fitted with an anti-handling device about which British bomb disposal knew very little and which a week earlier had killed an RAF officer attempting to disarm a similar device. Three times Babington attached a line to the head of the fuse to remove it, but each time the line broke. Although the device could have detonated at any moment, he kept trying and eventually succeeded and had the bomb lifted out and safely destroyed. His courage enabled bomb disposal teams to understand how to deal with the new device.

During the Coventry Blitz, 31-year-old Special Constable Brandon Moss went on duty every night despite having just worked a twelve-hour shift in a factory. On the night of 20–21 October, he led a rescue party to save three people trapped in a house in Clay Lane that had received a direct hit. Braving a gas leak and the threat of falling debris, when others retired to safety Moss kept going alone, tunnelling into the rubble to free the trio. He then learned that more people were trapped in a neighbouring house. Despite being exhausted – his rescue efforts eventually lasted from 11pm to 6.30am – and with a delayed-action bomb having fallen only 20ft away, he again worked alone and managed to free one person and recover four bodies. Moss became the first special constable to receive the George Cross.

Thirty-year-old Lieutenant Selby Armitage of the Royal Naval Volunteer Reserve was awarded the George Cross for his unstinting bravery in the autumn of 1940 when he defused a number of parachute mines, once climbing an unsteady ladder to attend to a mine that was found hanging from a tree in Orpington, Kent. When another on which he was working began ticking, Armitage had run less than 30 yards away before it exploded. Despite this near miss, he was back on duty next day. Armitage was one of only eight people to be awarded both the George Cross and George Medal, which he would receive in February 1944.

On 16 September 1940 Lieutenant-Commander Richard Ryan (37) and Chief Petty Officer Reginald Ellingworth (42) were the first bomb disposal men to deal with a new type of magnetic mine that had fallen on Clacton. When the first magnetic mines fell on London, the pair volunteered to make them safe. The bomb's clock was usually timed to go off 21 seconds after impact. If it failed to do so then the slightest movement could reactivate it. They dealt with six such mines, on one occasion working waist deep in mud and water in a canal, and on another making safe a mine that threatened an aerodrome and an explosives factory at Hornchurch. On 21 September, both men were killed when a mine hanging from a parachute in a warehouse exploded. They were each awarded the George Cross.

On 28 November 1940, Temporary Lieutenant Harold Newgass (41) was commanding a naval bomb disposal party making safe parachute mines on Merseyside. A mine had fallen through the roof of a gasometer in Garston. Its parachute had become entangled in the roof and so the mine had failed to explode. The gasometer held 2 million cubic feet of gas, half of Liverpool's supply. Some 1.25 million gallons of water had to be drained before, on 3 December, Newgass decided to tackle the job on his own. Because the air was unsafe he had to wear an oxygen cylinder that lasted only 30 minutes. He made six trips and was on his last cylinder before he could make the bomb safe. He received the George Cross.

In December 1940, 22-year-old Sub Lieutenant Francis Brooke-Smith disarmed a mine that had fallen on the deck of a fire-float on the Manchester Ship Canal. He was already an experienced bomb disposal officer but this presented him with particular difficulties; the mine was wedged awkwardly near the engine and he had to work purely by touch, using an unfamiliar piece of equipment. At one point, the clock began to tick but Brooke-Smith managed to stop it just in time. A month later, he disarmed an unstable bomb that was buried almost 6ft deep in an East London allotment. He received the George Cross.

Early in 1939, with war clouds gathering, government scientist, Arthur Merriman, had been working as Assistant Director Bomb Disposal with the Directorate of Scientific Research. In 1940, he was the Joint Secretary of the Unexploded Bomb Committee and travelled the country to research the situation, often pretending to be an air-raid warden because he liked to work under cover to see what was really happening. In the early hours of 11 September 1940, he did more than research. There was an unexploded 550lb bomb in London's Regent Street. The 47-year-old Merriman arrived on the scene just as the area had been evacuated. The bomb had started ticking but he began to remove its explosive material. When he felt the bomb was significantly safer, he withdrew. As a result of his bravery and expertise, when it exploded it caused minimal damage; only a few nearby windows were broken. He was awarded the George Cross, and soon afterwards was commissioned into the Royal Engineers.

On 8 September, the first day of the Blitz, 44-year-old Albert Dolphin was working as a porter at South-Eastern Hospital in New Cross, South London, when a bomb fell on the hospital's kitchens. Four nurses were killed and several others injured. Dolphin rushed to help one of the injured whose legs had been trapped by falling masonry. There was an ominous sound as another wall began to collapse. Although the rest of the would-be rescuers moved back, Dolphin flung himself over the nurse's body. Despite being severely injured she survived but Dolphin, a married man who had worked at the hospital for twenty years, was killed. For his selfless act he was awarded the George Cross.

On 19 October in Coventry, 17-year-old St John Ambulance cadet Betty Quinn, a stores clerk in her day job, was giving first-aid at an ARP post when a shower of incendiary bombs fell nearby. The *Coventry Standard* reported:

> 'She dealt with a number unaided. Bombs began to fall. A man was injured and she assisted him to a shelter. An Anderson shelter received a direct hit and she ran through a rain of bombs and commenced digging with a spade. She dug out seven persons and attended to their injuries. She returned to the post to assist distressed people.'

Betty had remained with the injured until the very last one had been removed by ambulance. For her courage she was awarded the George Medal.

Another 17-year-old, Rose Ede of Wadhurst in East Sussex, was awarded the George Medal after crawling into the ruins of a farmhouse that had been demolished by a German bomb. On 27 September 1940, she had gone out to investigate a bomb that had fallen on her vegetable patch, when another fell on a neighbouring home. Together with her father she ran to help. A child was still in its cot, which was perched on the edge of a bomb crater. Another was found nearby, but a third was buried. As her father lifted a beam, Rose crawled into the wreckage. After feeling around for almost half an hour she felt a foot, and a baby was pulled to safety. The three evacuee children were saved but their mother had been killed along with the farmer's wife. Rose said later, 'The sight of the wreckage is something I'll never forget. No one realises the damage a bomb can do until they see it … If I had thought about what I was doing, then perhaps I would have been afraid but I just went to the demolished building and that was it.'

Chapter Nineteen

A Filthy Crime

'The looters have systematically gone through the lot … stair carpets … they have even taken away heavy mangles, bedsteads and complete suites of furniture.'

Detective Inspector Percy Datlen,
Dover Borough Police

Of the fifty-six cases down for hearing at the Old Bailey on Tuesday, 15 November 1940, no fewer than twenty of them involved charges of looting premises damaged in recent air-raids. Worse still, ten of those cases involved members of the Auxiliary Fire Service. The war might have bred heroes but even among their ranks there were bad apples.

Later that week, Joseph Cowan (32), John Berwick (28), Reginald Edward Ledster (27), James Farrow (29), Arthur Francis Anderson (34) and Joseph Sparrowhawk (33) were each sentenced to five years' penal servitude after being found guilty of stealing property that had been left exposed by enemy bombing. Passing sentence, the Common Serjeant, Mr Cecil Whiteley KC, said:

'Since the declaration of war all of you have been full-time paid-up members of the AFS. That service was formed, equipped and trained for the express purpose of assisting the London Fire Brigade in the event of fires caused by enemy action. Each of you was sent to premises to extinguish fires or damp down debris.

'While so engaged, all of you seized the opportunity thus given to you of stealing stock on the premises that you could conveniently carry away in your buckets or your hands. You were about to drive away with the stolen property and return to your station when you were stopped owing to the vigilance of the police. It is a lamentable fact that it has been necessary to add to the many difficulties of the police force to watch members of your force. Sentence must be

severe. You have disgraced the uniform you wore and failed to carry
out the great traditions of the London Fire Brigade.'

As the sentences were announced, at the back of the court a woman burst
into tears and continued to sob as the men were taken down to the cells.

On the same day, four young soldiers – Noel Barton (19), Sidney Stuart
(17), William Lemmon (17) and William Edwards (17) – each pleaded
guilty at Thames Police Court in London to stealing money from gas
and electricity meters in premises damaged by bombing. Barton received
nine months' hard labour, Stuart and Lemmon each six months' hard
labour, and Edwards four months' hard labour.

Back at the Old Bailey, on 25 November war reserve policeman Frank
Henry Baughn (46) was found guilty of stealing three silver sweet dishes
and a silver mustard pot from a bomb-damaged house in Streatham
where the owner of the silverware, an elderly woman, had been killed
in the blast. Baughn was sentenced to five years' penal servitude. Forty-
year-old army deserter Samuel Levy received a similar sentence after
being found guilty of stealing a wireless set from a West End shop that
had been damaged by enemy action. The Recorder, Sir Gerald Dodson,
told Levy who had forty previous convictions, "I am satisfied that it was
a deliberate act of looting. You are a dangerous and plausible rogue.'

Sir Gerald – who was known in legal circles as 'The Wrecker' because
of the damage he did to the defence and who, four years later, would
preside over the trial of Forest Gate resident 72-year-old Jane Rebecca
Yorke, the last person to be convicted under the Witchcraft Act of
1735 – then found himself sentencing to two years' imprisonment, an
auxiliary fireman who had pleaded guilty to receiving tea and sugar from
warehouses attacked by the Luftwaffe. After sentencing the fireman,
Dodson turned his attention to the wider issue:

'Men in a position where temptation is often thrust upon them should
clearly understand that it has got to be resisted. It is particularly
grave when done by men who are paid to protect property. It is a
dreadful state of affairs and, unless it stops, sentences will increase
very rapidly.'

In the first eight weeks of the London Blitz, a total of 390 cases of looting were reported to the police. The war was becoming a golden age for the criminal class – men like army deserter Samuel Levy – but now it was not only the professional crooks that were taking advantage of the damage and confusion caused by the Blitz. People who might normally think of themselves as law-abiding citizens were now falling to the temptation of easy pickings.

In November, at a London court where 19-year-old Harry Stevens was fined £5 for stealing a bread plate from a store window that had been smashed by the blast from a bomb, the magistrate warned:

> 'An Englishman should not dream of committing an offence against a person suffering from German bombing and if anyone comes before me again in a flagrant case of looting I shall send him or her to prison for a long term.'

At Marylebone police court, 28-year-old George James Hanks was sentenced to nine months' hard labour for stealing raincoats, shoes and dress material from a railway goods depot when he should have been on duty as a fireman. Prosecuting solicitor Mr Harry Ricketts said, 'When bombs fall and everyone is taking cover, wholesale looting goes on upon every railway.' Detective Inspector Percy Datlen of Dover Borough Police reported that after one heavy raid on the town:

> 'In cases where there are several houses bombed out in one street, the looters have systematically gone through the lot. Carpets have been stripped from the floors, stair carpets have been removed; they have even taken away heavy mangles, bedsteads and complete suites of furniture.'

It was the same all over the country and it would only become worse. In March 1941, Mr Justice Charles would tell Leeds Assizes:

> 'In many cases these looters have operated on a wholesale scale. There were actually two men who had abandoned well-paid positions, one of them earning £7 to £9 a week, and work of public importance,

and who abandoned it to take up the obviously more remunerative occupation of looting.'

Age was no barrier either. At Humberside Police Court, a 76-year-old pensioner, William Spirit, was bound over for six months and ordered to pay 5s costs after he pleaded guilty to looting clothing worth 2s 6d from bombed premises. A 17-year-old from Leeds, Charles Edeson, was sent to prison for twenty-one days after admitting looting 28lb of lead piping. In December 1940, Sheffield Assizes set aside two days to deal with looters only. Among those charged were two soldiers, Robert Leslie Orlapp (22) of Bolton, and George Monteith (23) of Glasgow. A detective told the Sheffield court that the two men had been found drunk at the back of a shop. Cigars, ten rings, a wrist watch and other jewellery were found on them.

The same month, Mr H.R. Balmer, prosecuting a 25-year-old soldier charged with looting in Liverpool, told the court, 'On Friday we had more looting that ever before. There ghouls have been looting under the very eyes of the public and walking away with the booty while the blitz was still going on.' Cecil Roy Browning had been accused of stealing toothpaste and of being in unlawful possession of two packets of cigars, two cigarette cases, a pipe and a quantity of loose tobacco. Mr Balmer said, 'I am instructed to object to these alleged looters being allowed on bail. These men must be kept safely behind bars and locked up in these dangerous times.' All those charged with looting were denied bail that day.

In Coventry, three firemen were sentenced to six months' hard labour for stealing from a shop, and two men were caught red-handed ransacking a wine seller's shop in the middle of the 28 November air-raid. As he jailed them for six and seven years respectively, the judge told them, 'I cannot think of conduct more detestable than that, during the most dreadful air raid which has ever taken place, you should be found looting.'

As the Germans laid waste to Coventry, 28-year-old engineer, Edward Wilfred Critch, from Loughborough, was sentenced to three months' hard labour for stealing an eighteenth-century church register from the city's ruined cathedral. Detective-Constable William Sykes told Coventry magistrates that the Loughborough police had heard that

Sykes had the register, which was dated 1760, at his home. He had gone to Coventry 'for a bit of ARP experience' and had picked up the register for a souvenir. The chairman of the magistrates, Mrs Alderman Griffiths, told him, 'Coventry is passing through difficult days and it is not manly for people, to come here to collect souvenirs.' Critch was sentenced to three months' imprisonment with hard labour, as was a Coventry man, 29-year-old Colin Smith, who was found guilty of stealing elastic, lace, spoons, cotton and other articles from damaged premises. Smith, who was married with four children, told a policeman that he had bought them in a shop, but later changed his story, saying that he had found them in the street and was taking them to a police station. The *Yorkshire Evening Post* reported the case of a woman who removed a pair of shoes from a broken shop window 'with the thought that she would take them home to prevent someone stealing them'.

Gangs of children targeted gas and electricity meters in bomb-damaged houses, often directed by a Fagin-like figure. Between September 1940 and May 1941, juvenile crime accounted for almost half of all arrests and in those nine months there were 4,584 cases of looting. Understandably, victims were outraged. A letter writer to the *Sunderland Echo*, signing themselves 'Air-raid Victim', said:

> 'I would like to know the person who couldn't resist the temptation of stealing a sink from war-damaged property. It's a pity that the police can't catch these thieves in the act so that it would be a lesson to others. I am not just speaking for myself but other who have lost things the same way.'

After one raid, Joan Veazey, whose husband was a vicar in Kennington, south London, wrote in her diary, 'The most sickening thing was to see people like vultures, picking up things and taking them away. I didn't like to feel that English people would do this, but they did.' In November 1940, *The People* reported that the government was being urged to introduce the flogging of looters – '... the view taken is that the mentality of people who can commit this offence must be so depraved that only physical suffering can adequately punish them and deter others ...' – but the *Daily Mirror* went even further, telling readers of cases where 'ghouls

… rob even bodies lying in the ruins of little homes' and so 'hang a looter and stop this filthy crime'.

In fact, in November 1940, Osbert Peake, the MP for North Leeds and Under-Secretary of State for Home Affairs, promised that if looting increased then the death penalty would be invoked. A circular sent to magistrates reminded them of a recent statement by Peake, made in the House of Commons, in which he said that a 'stern view must be taken of such thefts'. The circular said that people convicted on indictment against the regulations were liable to sentence of death or penal servitude. The same week the Metropolitan Police commissioner, Sir Philip Game, announced that the force's special squad to track looters had been enlarged and that he had told his men that looting had to stop. Steps were also being taken through local authorities to speed up at least the partial salvage from damaged buildings.

However, while the general public might have despised looters, it was only one element of a soaring wartime crime rate. Between 1939 and 1945, reported crimes in England and Wales rose from 303,711 to 478,394, an increase of 57 per cent. There were now many more laws, rules and regulations to break. Rationing meant that there was soon a flourishing black market, while there were what we would today call 'benefit cheats'. People who had lost their homes through bombing were entitled to a payment of £500 and, in addition, they could claim compensation for family or personal items lost through enemy action. One enterprising young man, Walter Handy of Wandsworth, was given a three-year prison sentence for falsely claiming to have been bombed out no less than nineteen times in five months. At the height of the bombing, National Assistance Office staff did not have the time or the resources to check every claim that houses had become uninhabitable and that furniture, clothes and ration books had been destroyed in air-raids. Handy seems to have eventually been caught simply because he overdid it. In 1941, additional staff were brought in to check more thoroughly.

Another major fraud centred on billeting. The government paid 10s 6d for taking in a child evacuee and a further 8s 6d per head if more than one was taken in. It did not take long for some people to see this as a way of increasing their income and not always lawfully. Some continued to claim their allowances after their guests had returned home. Others stole blank billeting forms and completed them in order that allowances could be drawn for non-existent people.

In January 1940, two married women appeared before Hitchin Sessions, each accused of drawing billeting scheme money to which they were not entitled. Dorothy Grace Pickett (32) was charged in respect of £3 16s 6d but the solicitor prosecuting on behalf of the Ministry of Health said that the defendant had actually obtained £6 7s 6d by fraud but that the Post Office employees that he would have called as witnesses were now serving in the armed forces. The court was told that in November 1939, Mrs Pickett said that she had lost her original billeting form and a duplicate was issued. She then presented two forms at different Post Offices to obtain five double payments in respect of three children. She pleaded guilty and after the court was told that she had repaid two sums of 5s and 7s 6d respectively, she was fined £5.

The second woman, Christine Tracey, was charged with fraudulently obtaining £4 after continuing to claim for a mother and three children who had left her home after being billeted there for less than a month. Mrs Tracey told the court, 'The reason I did this was because my husband was out of work, our income was £1 8s 0d and the rent was £1. I was short of food.' She told the court that her husband was now in work, earning £2 5s per week. She was also fined £5.

Some frauds made even more imaginative use of wartime regulations. A Bromsgrove court was told how a 32-year-old soldier, Selby Hector Purves, had impersonated an army billeting officer and attempted to obtain by fraud a quantity of provisions said to be required for military purposes. He had also posed as a lieutenant qualified to act as a billeting officer when, in fact, he was a private absent without leave from his regimental depot in Scotland. Purves promised people who did not want to provide billets for soldiers that upon payment of £1 per man they would be exempt.

Even these offences seemed small fry when he told the court about other schemes upon which he had embarked. Before the war, he and other men working on the construction of military buildings had been obtaining money by clocking-on to jobs, then working elsewhere and drawing pay from both sources. After the outbreak of war, he and his friends set up a scheme to obtain money from young men of rich families who wished to avoid military service. After contacting the men, they set up meetings in Horse Guards Parade: 'One of us would go into the building, and as we were dressed as officers, the sentries would salute us, and this would give the young fellow with us a sense of security. We would afterwards go into a small café and assure the young fellow that providing he paid sums varying from £25 to £100, according to his means, then his name would be forgotten on the calling-up list, Several were fools enough to take it on.'

Purves had also tried to obtain horses – including one called Don Bradman that had run in the 1937 Grand National – allegedly for Army remounts. He had been offered £150 to get Don Bradman to a pre-arranged meeting place but the owner, George Jackson, had become suspicious and called the police.

'We were trying to do too much and made a mess of it,' Purves told the court. Superintendent Price thought that this frank statement, making a clean breast of everything, had actually been made with the object of gaining notoriety. In 1931, Purves had given himself up to police after confessing to the murder of a girl in Epsom. He had not committed the crime, although he had once been imprisoned for attempting to murder an NCO in India. For these latest crimes, in January 1940, he received the remarkably lenient sentences, for the times, of nine months' imprisonment.

Late in 1940, there were several instances of thieves preying on people who spent their nights in air-raid shelters. Handbags and the contents of suitcases were targeted. Although by the following year so-called 'shelter gangs' were perfecting a dark art introduced by lone opportunist thieves, mob rule had already taken hold in 1940. In October, one man had asked the police to intervene when the private shelter that he provided for his workers was taken over by a 'mob of gangsters' who terrified others seeking shelter to the extent that they were too frightened to identify the men. The police said that they could not intervene on private premises. The problem worsened and in December, shelter marshals were asking for legal powers to evict 'unruly shelterers', although the same month a shelter marshal in London was found harbouring Canadian army deserters on his premises. Kenneth John Good, an 18-year-old storeman, was in charge of a shelter where police found seven men, one of whom had changed into civilian clothes and was in possession of a false identity card. Bow Street police court fined Good £5 for assisting a soldier to desert from his regiment.

There was, though, a certain acceptance of many of the offences and sharp practices that the war had brought. While maximum price controls had been introduced to prevent businesses from profiteering, in the normal run of events people did not mind paying extra – if they could afford it, of course – for food and other items that were in short supply. In January 1940, the writer Horace Annesley Vachell said that apart from the carnage:

'war is loathed because it dislocates life ... a paternal government is controlling profiteering; and the general public has been invited to report even small overcharges to authority. Many of us, rich or poor alike, are too indolent or possibly too busy to accept this wise invitation. We attempt to grin and bear what has become humorously termed "collateral slaps of Providence".'

In December 1940, husband and wife, Francis and Hilda Upton appeared at Hailsham police court accused of having in their possession on 19 September more than one ration book each. The manager of the local Co-operative store told the court that the defendants had first produced ration books that had been issued at Hailsham and later books that had been issued at Camberwell. Mr Upton said that he sometimes stayed in London while his wife remained in Polegate in East Sussex. As he moved from one district to another he thought he needed to register in both places. He had never had double rations. Nonetheless, each was fined £2.

Ration books were certainly causing problems for some people. In October, Hartlepool magistrates were occupied for a whole morning hearing food prosecution summonses against one family. Grace Davison was fined £1 plus costs after being found guilty of obtaining rationed sugar for household consumption in excess of the amount prescribed.

Robert Davison of the same address was fined £1 and costs for altering without lawful authority two ration books in the names of Mary Dixon and Irene Collins. Mrs Dixon had been employed by Mrs Davison as a charwoman and it was customary for her to have breakfast, dinner and a cup of tea at the Davisons, while Irene Collins worked there as a day girl, and she too had breakfast, dinner and sometimes tea at the house. It appeared that the Davisons did not know that their two servants had separate ration books at other addresses. The Northern Regional Ministry of Food Office had brought the cases. Another Hartlepool woman was fined for using four ration books to get food for her family of three. The Ministry of Food had mistakenly sent her 15-year-old son both a child's ration book and an adult's. For six months she had used both books to obtain additional supplies, claiming that she thought the extra rations were because her son was a 'big schoolboy'. The system was difficult to monitor. People used ration books belonging to relatives who had died. Others simply exchanged with their neighbours and friends rations they did not want.

Despite what people might like to tell themselves, offences such as benefit and ration book fraud were not 'victimless' crimes, but many people could perhaps understand them. It was the blackouts and bombings that were obviously going to provide greater opportunities for those inclined not only to steal but also to rape and murder. The blackout was proving a boon not only to thieves, especially pickpockets, but also to those with more sinister motives still. In January 1940, a 14-year-old boy appeared before a Cornish juvenile court after indecently assaulting a woman in a Newlyn street. He admitted several other similar offences including that of assaulting a young girl on a footpath. He had started out, he said, simply by using the excuse of the blackout to bump into women, before moving on to assaulting them. His father was bound over in the sum of £5 to see that the boy was of good behaviour. 'This is a serious offence and we are going to protect the public more particularly during the blackout,' magistrate Graham H. Bennett told the court.

Another assault, however, ended in tragedy. At around 7.45pm on Saturday, 16 November 1940, 17-year-old grocery shop manageress Minnie Stott said goodbye to her father, Fred, and left her home in Clarence Street, Bolton. At about 8pm she called into the United Cow

Products restaurant on Deansgate where her mother, Alice, worked as a waitress. She told Alice that she was going to the cinema. Fred and Alice never saw their daughter alive again. Just before midnight, PC Harry Brooks found her body in a secluded yard on Bradshawgate. She had been sexually assaulted and strangled. The police had few details to work on. One suspect – a soldier who had a drink with Minnie in the Founders Arms two days earlier – was quickly eliminated, but when her devastated parents visited her grave at Heaton cemetery on 12 January 1941 a woman approached them and said that their daughter had been with two girls on the night she was murdered. The woman claimed that two men had forced Minnie into their car as the other two girls fled. The girls and men in the car were never found. Like most towns and cities, in 1940 Bolton was teeming with servicemen, most of them strangers. The murder of Minnie Stott remains one of the many unsolved crimes committed in blacked-out wartime Britain.

Chapter Twenty

Canopied With Uncertainties

'… Grim, indeed, 1940 has been, but we have more than survived …'
Right Reverend Benjamin Pollard,
Bishop of Lancaster

On 6 November 1940, Willie Gallacher, the Communist MP for Fife West, asked in the House of Commons if the Parliamentary Secretary to the Ministry of Food was aware that on 1 October some 2,500 bunches of bananas in good condition had been loaded into barges and disposed of at sea and whether he would prosecute those responsible. The reply came from the Parliamentary Secretary to the Board of Trade, Major Gwylim Lloyd George, the Independent Liberal MP for Pembrokeshire and a younger son of David Lloyd George. He said that the bananas had been found to be quite unfit for human consumption and had been condemned by the medical officer of health. So the latter part of the question did not arise.

Bananas were about to become a touchy subject in Britain. Up until now the fruit had been freely available, even in wartime. By December 1940, daily market prices showed them selling at about twopence each – as opposed to the one-shilling cost of a cucumber – and newspapers and magazines were full of recipes that used bananas as an ingredient. Mashed up with the white of an egg they apparently made a tolerable substitute for fresh cream. On 2 November, there was good news; generous shipping space had been allocated by the Ministry of Food to import more Jamaican bananas. The Ministry would also purchase Jamaica's entire orange crop. But then, on 19 November, Sir John Mellor, Conservative MP for Tamworth, asked the Ministry:

'Why, having regard to their bulky and perishable nature, the continued import of bananas is permitted at a time when it has been considered necessary to ration tea and sugar in order to save shipping space and exchange reserves?'

Sir John had a point and it was one that was well received. The following week, Ronald Cross (Conservative, Rossendale), the Minister of Shipping, revealed that Britain's shipping losses had risen to 60,000 tons per week. Ronald Cross and Sir John Mellor were on the same page; bananas were 'a bulky cargo, taking up much more shipping space than other equally good foods require'. Although 60,000 tons a week was 'only' about equal to the average sunk by enemy action during the last war, it provided, said Cross, the reason why bananas had now been banned.

Such a ban would hit Jamaica hard – in 1938, the country had exported almost £3 million-worth of bananas to Britain and no other market could begin to compensate her for the loss. Elders and Fyffes, the main importers of bananas, said that the Colonial Office had told the firm that no more licences to bring the fruit into Britain would be issued, effective immediately. Present stocks would last for two weeks and as there were ships already loaded and licensed there would be supplies until probably 22 December, so there would still be bananas this Christmas; but next year? It was another sign – albeit utterly trivial compared to the horrors that were being visited upon the civilian population – that the war was now biting hard.

The second Christmas of the Second World War was quite unlike the first, when life had continued much as before, when a shortage of bananas would never have been countenanced. A year that had begun during a Phoney War, when the Nazis occupied only Poland and Czechoslovakia, had ended with the Blitz. In between, there had been the German occupation of Denmark and Norway, the fall of France and the Low Countries, the evacuation from Dunkirk, the threat of invasion, and the Battle of Britain. Many town and city centres across Britain now lay in ruins. The likelihood of death or at least serious injury was now a constant companion. On Christmas Eve, people were still choosing to spend the night in their shelters, not least in cities such as Manchester where there were air-raids even on the 24th. Yet in the run-up to Christmas, people still did their best to cling on to whatever normality they could. In Manchester, Christmas shopping at Lewis's was in full swing:

'On the first floor is the vast Toy Fair – a wonderland for all children
– and Father Christmas himself in his Nursery Rhyme Grotto
(free) in the Basement.'

The war, though, was never far from anyone's thoughts, even when they
were trying to sell confectionery. In the *Manchester Evening News,* an
advertisement for Caley's Fortune chocolates carried a sketch representing
a female ambulance driver 'who needs lots of pluck and nerves of steel.
Often she has a pretty grim time but she hasn't lost her taste for nice
things. Try her with a box of Fortune. She will love these best of all ...'
Adults were advised to keep a flask of Black and White whisky by them in
order to ward off 'air-raid chills'. On the same page was news that Salford
wanted paid shelter stewards and that Miss Ellen Wilkinson, the Labour
MP for Jarrow, and a junior minister at the Ministry of Home Security,
had arranged to see for herself how Salford slept in the shelters.

In Birmingham, Cook's of Bull Street offered 'a brochure that puts
before you candidly the dos and don'ts of safe wartime furnishing'.
There might be a war on but the people of Birmingham could still
furnish a beautiful home in time for Christmas. Just in case anyone had
forgotten the bigger issues, the local Midland Red bus company asked the
public not to travel between 7am and 9am, and 4.30pm and 7pm, unless
their work was of national importance. 'Our appeals have met with some
response but, like Oliver Twist, we want more!'

The Bon Marché store in Liverpool still had a small stock of silk
stockings – rumoured to soon become unavailable – ranging from 3s 6d
to 7s 4d a pair, and there were 'gay string and felt gloves' at 5s 6d and
7s 11d a pair, and sheepskin slippers from 12s 9d, while in the store's
restaurant, Joseph Greene, 'the pianist with a European reputation' was
giving a 'celebrity concert' daily at 3pm. Although bananas were about to
disappear from the shops, the *Liverpool Evening Express* marvelled at the
fact that Britain had been at war for more than twelve months, yet here
were still well-stocked stores displaying hundreds of interesting items.
There was, said the newspaper, 'nothing approaching Mother Hubbard's
cupboard so far as Liverpool is concerned'. It suggested that umbrellas
with torches on their handles would make an excellent gift, just right for
getting around in the blackout during a rain shower.

Despite many of the shared experiences that the war had brought about, there really was still a huge class division in Britain and this was nowhere more apparent than when it came to shopping. For the less well-off, life had become much harder; for the more fortunate members of society the sacrifices were not as great, although the risks to life and limb obviously were. Writing in the magazine *Britannia and Eve*, C. Patrick Thompson thought that Christmas 1940 would be, in general, 'canopied with uncertainties' although 'one thing is certain – it will not be a turkey and champagne Christmas, but a home-grown roast beef and beer Christmas'. Thousands of people who had been bombed out of their homes would have gladly settled for that. Thompson wrote of shops advertising a mink coat for £400, '… There seems to be a good deal of the "If we're going to be bombed tomorrow, you may as well buy me a fur, and a good one, today".'

The People newspaper had another idea:

'Why not send War Savings Certificates or National Savings Gift Tokens. Buy them at any Post Office. They will save you and the postman trouble, give a lot of pleasure, and help win the war. Of course, you can also buy Postal Orders.'

The National Savings Committee had in 1940 promoted a series of War Weapons Weeks in towns and cities. In each case, the amount raised by the sale of War Bonds would be added to the total for War Savings Certificates and Defence Bonds, and by deposits in the Post Office and Trustee savings banks in that week. For the rest of the war, various schemes such as Warships Week and Spitfire Fund all raised money. Warships Weeks alone would contribute over £955 million to the national need. There were other appeals, this time not to raise money for arms but to help victims of the Blitz. As the year ended, newspapers across the country carried an appeal by the Lord Mayor's National Air Raid Distress Fund, launched from the Mansion House in London. The message was:

'On a hot Saturday afternoon [in] September 1940 German bombers flew over Britain destroying man and his possessions … destruction by that cowardly means continue and will endure … to share the burden of suffering will be the wish of every man and woman in Britain.'

From twilight to full-on searchlight, from the occupation of the Channel Islands to the threat of the invasion of mainland Britain itself, through the Battle of Britain and the Blitz – surely no British generation had ever lived through such a single year? On New Year's Eve, the Bishop of Lancaster, the Right Reverend Benjamin Pollard, addressed his flock:

'... Grim, indeed, 1940 has been, but we have more than survived and ... the climax of the war will probably come in 1941, and we shall need all the unity, courage and faith we can muster to beat down the evil and implacable foe ...'

Bibliography

Books

Calder, Angus, *The Myth of the Blitz*, Pimlico, 1992

Geraghty, T., *A North-East Coastal Town: Ordeal and Triumph*, Kingston upon Hill Corporation, 1951

Haining, Peter, *Spitfire Summer*, W.H. Allen, 1990

Kirkham, Pat and Thoms, David (editors) *War Culture: Social Change and Changing Experience in World War Two*, Lawrence & Wishart, 1995

Minton, Michael, *Heroes of the Birmingham Air Raids*, Brewin Books, 2002

Nicholson, Harold, *Diaries and Letters 1939–45*, William Collins, Sons and Co Ltd, 1967

Rippon, Anton, *Gas Masks for Goalposts*, Sutton, 2005

Rippon, Anton, *How Britain Kept Calm and Carried On*, Michael O'Mara Books, 2014

Saville, John, *Insane and Unseemly*, Matador, 2009

Stansky, Peter, *The First Day of the Blitz*, Yale University Press, 2007

Wallington, Neil, *Firemen at War: The Work of London's Firefighters in the Second World War*, Jeremy Mills Publishing, 2007

Newspapers and Journals

Aberdeen Press and Journal
Bedfordshire Times and Independent
BBC Year Book
(Birmingham) *Evening Despatch*
Birmingham Gazette
Birmingham Mail
(Birmingham) *Sports Argus*
Britannia and Eve
Coventry Evening Telegraph
Coventry Standard
Daily Dispatch
Daily Express
Daily Herald
Daily Mail
Daily Mirror
Daily Sketch
Daily Worker
Derby Evening Telegraph
Dover Express and East Kent News
Dundee Courier
(Exeter) *Express and Echo*
Gloucestershire Echo
Hull Daily Mail
Illustrated
Lancashire Evening Post
Liverpool Daily Post
Liverpool Echo
Liverpool Evening Express
Manchester Evening News
Manchester Guardian
New York Herald Tribune
New York Sun

Newcastle Evening Chronicle
Newcastle Weekly Chronicle
News Review
North-Eastern Daily Gazette
Northern Whig
Nottingham Evening Post
Nottingham Journal
Penrith Observer
Portsmouth Evening News
Punch, Radio Times
Sheffield Star
Sheffield Telegraph
Staffordshire Sentinel

Sunday Pictorial
Sunderland Echo
The Bystander
The Cricketer
The New Yorker
The People
The Scotsman
The Times
Theatre World
Western Daily Press
Western Morning News
Wisden Cricketers' Almanack
Yorkshire Evening Post

Index